ıu

A Bandwidth-Efficient

or

Filtering

A. P. Thanga Muthu

A Bandwidth-Efficient Cooperative Authentication Scheme for Filtering

Injected False Data in Wireless Sensor Networks

LAP LAMBERT Academic Publishing

Imprint

Any brand names and product names mentioned in this book are subject to trademark, brand or patent protection and are trademarks or registered trademarks of their respective holders. The use of brand names, product names, common names, trade names, product descriptions etc. even without a particular marking in this work is in no way to be construed to mean that such names may be regarded as unrestricted in respect of trademark and brand protection legislation and could thus be used by anyone.

Cover image: www.ingimage.com

Publisher:
LAP LAMBERT Academic Publishing
is a trademark of
International Book Market Service Ltd., member of OmniScriptum Publishing Group
17 Meldrum Street, Beau Bassin 71504, Mauritius

Printed at: see last page
ISBN: 978-620-0-49966-0

Content:

development process. Before developing the tool it is necessary to determine the time factor, economy n company strength. Once these things r satisfied, ten next steps is to determine which operating system and language can be used for developing the tool. Once the programmers start building the tool the programmers need lot of external support. This support can be obtained from senior programmers, from book or from websites. Before building the system the above consideration r taken into account for developing the proposed system.

Literature survey is the most important step in software development process. Before developing the tool it is necessary to determine the time factor, economy n company strength. Once these things r satisfied, ten next steps is to determine which operating system and language can be used for developing the tool. Once the programmers start building the tool the programmers need lot of external support. This support can be obtained from senior programmers, from book or from websites. Before building the system the above consideration r taken into account for developing the proposed system.

The analysis of Parallel and distributed systems Survey is as follows:

Parallel and distributed computing

1. "A distributed system is a collection of independent computers that appear to the users of the system as a single computer."
2. "A distributed system consists of a collection of autonomous computers linked to a computer network and equipped with distributed system software."
3. "A distributed system is a collection of processors that do not share memory or a clock."
4. "Distributed systems are a term used to define a wide range of computer systems from a weakly-coupled system such as wide area networks, to very strongly coupled systems such as multiprocessor systems."

Distributed systems are groups of networked computers, which have the same goal for their work. The terms "concurrent computing", "parallel computing", and "distributed computing" have a lot of overlap, and no clear distinction exists between them. The same system may be characterized both as "parallel" and "distributed"; the processors in a typical distributed system run concurrently in parallel. Parallel computing may be seen as a particular tightly-coupled form of distributed computing, and distributed computing may be seen as a loosely-coupled form of parallel computing. Nevertheless, it is possible to roughly classify concurrent systems as "parallel" or "distributed" using the following criteria:

- In parallel computing, all processors have access to a shared memory. Shared memory can be used to exchange information between processors.

In distributed computing, each processor has its own private memory (distributed memory). Information is exchanged by passing messages between the processors

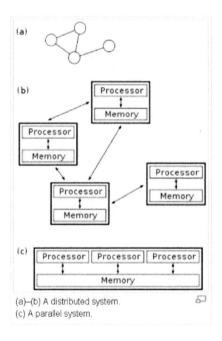

(a)–(b) A distributed system.
(c) A parallel system.

Fig4. Processing of Data memory allocation

The figure on the right illustrates the difference between distributed and parallel systems. Figure (a) is a schematic view of a typical distributed system; as usual, the system is represented as a network topology in which each node is a computer and each line connecting the nodes is a communication link. Figure (b) shows the same distributed system in more detail: each computer has its own local memory, and information can be exchanged only by

Proposed Methodology

The design goal of proposed system is to achieve bandwidth-efficient authentication for filtering injected false data. Every sensor node in wireless sensor network shares a private key with the sink.Each node knows its one-hop neighbors and establish a public-private key pair with each of them.

In this scheme it use Message Authentication Code (MAC) mechanism to authenticate broadcast messages and every node can verify the broadcast messages.Each MAC is set to 1 bit to achieve bandwidth efficient authentication. To filter the false data injected by attacked sensor nodes, the BECAN scheme adopts cooperative neighbor router (CNR)-based filtering mechanisms in figure 6 .

Here a source node N0 is ready to send a report m to the sink via an established routing path PN0: {P1 – P2 ...Pl – Sink}, it first resorts to its k neighboring sensor nodes SN0 : {S1,S2, . . .,S$_k$} to cooperatively authenticate the report m, and then sends it together with the authentication information MAC from N0 to the sink via routing RN0, where the sink initializes all sensor nodes, then each one of it shares its private key with the sink.

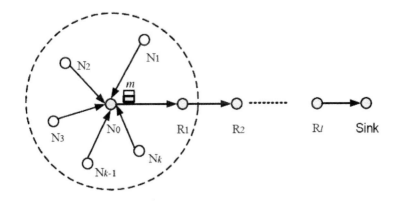

Fig6.Data applying the nodes

With this mechanism BECAN calculate the probability of k-neighbors, which provides the necessary condition needed for BECAN authentication. With the proposed mechanism, injected false data can be early detected and filtered by the en-route sensor nodes if there is at least one uncompromised neighboring node participating in the reporting. In addition, the accompanied authentication information is bandwidth-efficient.

Finally develop a custom Java simulator to demonstrate the effectiveness of the proposed BECAN scheme in terms of en-routing filtering probability and false negative rate on true reportstication. Various false data filtering mechanisms have been developed, since most of these filtering mechanisms use the symmetric key technique were the compromised node can abuse its keys to generate false reports, and the reliability of the filtering mechanisms will be degraded.

The proposed mechanism can save energy by early detecting and filtering the majority of injected false data. Therefore, it is important to share the authentication tasks with the en-route sensor nodes such that the injected false data is detected and discarded earlier. If the injected false data is detected in network as soon as possible, the more energy can be saved from the whole network with only very little extra overhead at enroute nodes.Henceonly small amount of injected false data needs to be verified by the head sink, which thus largely is reducing its burden. Since the sensor nodes are less costly, it is desirable to design a bandwidth efficient authentication scheme Compared with the previously reported mechanisms, this new mechanism achieves not only high filtering probability but also high reliability. i.e., even though some of the sensor nodes are compromised, obviously the actual reports generated will reach the *sink* with high probability.

To filter the false data injected by compromised sensor nodes, the BECAN adopts cooperative neighbor x router (CNR)-based filtering mechanism.

When a source node N0 is ready to send a report m to the sink via an established routing path it first resorts to its k neighboring nodes NN0 : {N1, N2, . . ., N_k} to cooperatively authenticate the report m, and then sends the report m and the authentication information MAC from N0 U NN0 to the sink via routing RN0 , where each mac_{ij}, $0 \leq i \leq k$, $1 \leq j \leq l$, represents Ni's MAC on m for R_j's authentication, and each mac_{is} represents Ni's MAC on m for the sink's authentication. As indicated in network model, the sink initializes all sensor nodes, and then each sensor node shares its private key with the sink.

factors. For elliptic-curve-based protocols, it is assumed that finding the discrete logarithm of a random elliptic curve element with respect to a publicly-known base point is infeasible. The size of the elliptic curve determines the difficulty of the problem. It is believed that the same level of security afforded by an RSA-based system with a large modulus can be achieved with a much smaller elliptic curve group. Using a small group reduces storage and transmission requirements.

Let p be a large prime and $E(IFp)$ represent an elliptic curve defined over IF_p. Let G $\in E(IFp)$ be a base point of prime order q. Then, each sensor node $Ni \in N$ can preload a TinyECC based public-private key pair (Yi, xi), where the private key xi is randomly chosen from Z^*q and the public key $Y_i = X_i$, G. No interactive key pair establishment. For any two sensor nodes vi, $vj \in G = (V,\acute{\epsilon})$ no matter what $eij \in \{0,1\}$ is, sensor nodes vi with the key pair (Yi, xi) and vj with the key pair (Y_j, X_j) can establish a secure Elliptic Curve Diffie-Hellman (ECDH) key pair without direct contacting, where $k_{ij}=x_iY_j=x_ix_jg=x_ix_jg=x_ix_jy_i=k_{ji}$. v_i and v_j can secretly share a key. At the same time, the established keys are independent. In other words, if a sensor node vi is compromised, then the key k_{ij} shared between v_i and v_j will be disclosed. However, the key k_{ij} shared between v_j and another sensor node v_j` is not affected.

G.Design Rationale

To filter the false data injected by compromised sensor nodes, the BECAN adopts cooperative neighbor router (CNR) based filtering mechanism. As shown in Fig.6 CNR-based mechanism, when a source node N0 is ready to send a report m to the sink via an established routing path RN0: [R1 -> R2 ->. .Rl-> Sink], it first resorts to its k neighboring nodes NN0: {N1, N2, . ..,Nk} to cooperatively authenticate the report m, and then sends the report m and the authentication information MAC from N0 U NN0 to the sink via routing RN0.

CHAPTER IV

IMPLEMETATION

This chapter deals with Practical design and implementation issues in building the proposed mechanism.

A. Sensor node initialization and deployment

The base station (sink), forwarding node and sensor nodes has been designed the sink deploys these initialized sensor nodes at a Certain Interest Region (CIR). It is assumed that all sensor nodes are uniformly distributed in CIR after deployment. Sink initializes sensor nodes with unique id.Sensor node chooses a private key from key pool and share with sink. The sensor node, which senses an event, will be chosen as the cluster head.

B. Routing establishment

Forwarding node and sensor nodes has been designed. Base station receives message from sensor node. While establishing sensor node, the system identifies the cluster head, which is also one of the sensor node. Sensor node always sends data via cluster head, then to forwarding node and then to base station. For this sensor node and forwarding nodes must establish their neighbor nodes automatically. When these sensor nodes do not have the reporting task, they will establish the route to sink using the shortest path. They also try to adapt a routing path based on some existing routing protocol. This established routing path can speed up the reporting. As soon as an event occurs, a report is immediately delivered along this routing path.

C. Sensed Results Reporting Protocol

To filter the false data injected by compromised sensor nodes, the BECAN scheme adopts cooperative neighbor router (CNR)-based filtering mechanism. In the CNR-based mechanism, when a sensor(source)node N0 has sensed some data m and is ready to report m to the sink via the routing path RN0: {R1 - R2 ...Rl – Sink}. The source node N0 gains the current timestamp T, chooses k neighboring nodes NN0 : {N1,N2, . . .,Nk} and sends the report m. The source node N0 use key pair establishment to compute shared keys with each node in {N0, N1,N2, ..,Nk} as {k01, k02...k0l,k0s}.if Ni believes the report m is true then add MAC information with report send to sink along routing path .

D. Filtering false injection attack

When each sensor node R_i, along the routing RN0 receives message m, timestamp T, and MAC key from its upstream node, it checks the integrity of the message m and the timestamp T. If the timestamp T is out of date, the received message m, timestamp T and MAC key will be discarded. Otherwise, R_i accepts the data will forward the message (m, T, MAC) to its downstream node, Otherwise, (m,T,MAC) will be discarded.

E.Sink Verification

Sink receives report m, Timestamp and MAC. Check the time, if the timestamp is unmatched or old, then the report will be discarded. Next the sink then check the MAC information if correct sink accepts the report m else reject. The BECAN scheme introduces Multireports solution to provide high reliability. As shown in below figure, once an event occurs, multi sensor nodes near to event freely choose different neighbors then the reports are delivered to sink through different established paths. If one report reaches the sink correctly, it will be successfully reported. That's how reliability of the BECAN scheme improved.

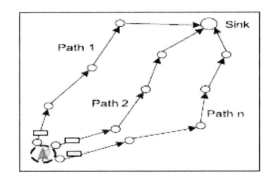

Fig9. Data path selection based transmitting

BECAN Scheme also resolves the scalability problem. The devise a large sensor network is divided into a heterogeneous sensor network .In each one consists of a powerful High-end sensor (Hsensor) acting as Cluster Head and a number of Low-end sensors (L-sensors), as shown in below figure. L-sensor senses tevent send report to the neighboring H-sensor.

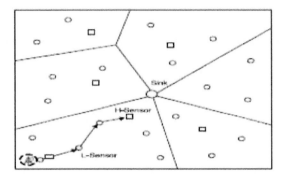

Fig10. Clustering and data check sensor

Energy saving is always crucial for the lifetime of wireless sensor networks. In this section, the performance of the proposed BECAN scheme is evaluated in terms of energy efficiency.

Energy Consumption in Non-interactive Key-pair Establishments

The proposed BECAN method has added computational cost because of expensive ECDH operations at the time of establishment of non-interactive key pair. Fortunately, since the non-interactive key pair establishments are averagely distributed in each sensor node and only executed once during the routing establishment, the ECDH operation is not a heavy burden. In order to achieve same amount of security as 1024 bit RSA, we can consider 160 bit elliptic curve during the design of TinyECC based sensor node [25]. Assume that, each sensor node is equipped with a low-power high performance sensor platform, i.e., MICAz [21]. Then, according to [19], this type of sensor platform only requires 50.82 mJ to establish a non-interactive shared key.

Energy Consumption in Transmission

The majority of injected false data can be filtered by BECAN within 15 hops during transmission. Thus, BECAN can greatly save the energy of sensor nodes along the routing path. In order to quantitatively measure the energy saving in BECAN, we compare the energy consumption of BECAN with that of SEF within the length of routing path H = 15 hops. For fair comparison, we set the parameter k = 4, and 0, three among four neighboring nodes colluding with the compromised source node N0, which corresponds to Nc = 1, 4 with T = 5 in SEF [9]. Because SEF does not consider the compromise of enrooting nodes, we also set ρ = 0 in BECAN.

Implementation is the stage of the project when the theoretical design is turned out into a working system. Thus it can be considered to be the most critical stage in achieving a successful new system and in giving the user, confidence that the new system will work and be effective.

The implementation stage involves careful planning, investigation of the existing system and it's constraints on implementation, designing of methods to achieve changeover and evaluation of changeover methods.

Algorithm   CNR Based MAC Generation

1: **procedure** CNRBASEDMACGENERATION
   Input: $params$, $N_i \in (N_{N_0} \cup N_0)$, m, T, R_{N_0}
   Output: Row_i
2:   N_i uses the non-interactive keypair establishment to compute shared keys with each node in $R_{N_0} : [R_1 \rightarrow R_2 \rightarrow \cdots \rightarrow R_l \rightarrow Sink]$ as $k_{i1}, k_{i2}, \cdots, k_{il}, k_{is}$, where k_{is} is N_i's private key distributed by the $sink$
3:   **if** N_i believes the report m is true **then**   ▷ a neighboring node is assumed having the same ability to detect a true event as the source node and correctly judge the report m.

1. BECAN Scheme

A novel bandwidth-efficient cooperative authentication (BECAN) scheme for filtering injected false data in wireless sensor networks. Compared with the previously reported mechanisms, the BECAN scheme achieves not only high filtering probability but also high reliability.

•) First, we study the random graph characteristics of wireless sensor node deployment, and estimate the probability of k-neighbors, which provides the necessary condition for BECAN authentication;

•) Second, we propose the BECAN scheme to filter the injected false data with cooperative bit-compressed authentication technique. With the proposed mechanism, injected false data can be early detected and filtered by the en-route sensor nodes. In addition, the accompanied authentication information is bandwidth-efficient; and

•) Third, we develop a custom simulator to demonstrate the effectiveness of the proposed BECAN scheme in terms of en-routing filtering probability and false negative rate on true reports.

2. Early detecting the injected false data by the en-route sensor nodes

The *sink* is a powerful data collection device. Nevertheless, if all authentication tasks are fulfilled at the *sink*, it is undoubted that the *sink* becomes a bottleneck. At the same time, if too many injected false data flood into the *sink*, the *sink* will surly suffer from the Denial of Service (DoS) attack. Therefore, it is critical to share the authentication tasks with the en-route sensor nodes such that the injected false data can be detected and discarded early. The earlier the injected false data are detected, the more energy can be saved in the whole network.

3. Gang Injecting False Data Attack

We introduce a new stronger injecting false data attack, called gang injecting false data attack, in wireless sensor networks. This kind of attack is usually launched by a gang of compromised sensor nodes controlled and moved by an adversary A. As shown in Fig. 2, when a compromised source node is ready to send a false data, several compromised nodes will first move and aggregate at the source node, and then collude to inject the false data. Because of the mobility, the gang injecting false data attack is more challenging and hard to resist.

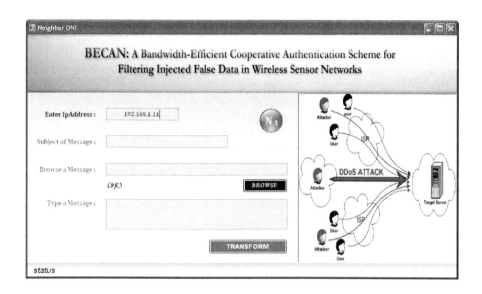

Fig11. I/P applying node 1

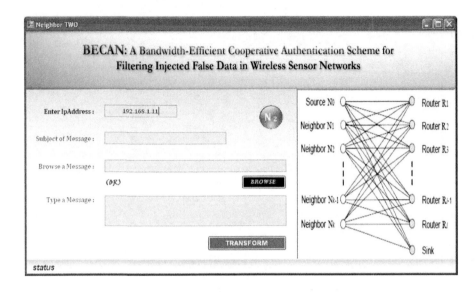

Fig12. I/P applying node 2

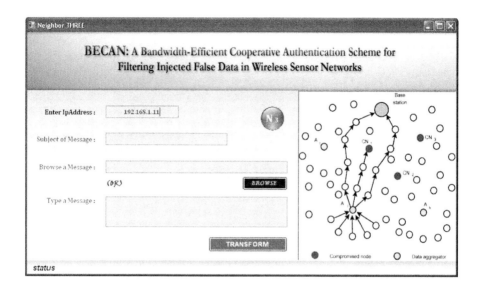

Fig13. I/P applying node S

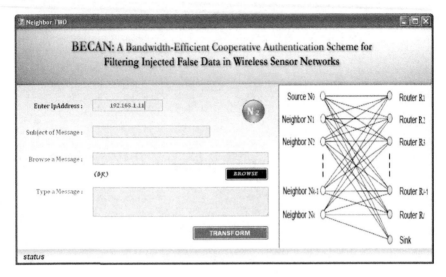

Fig14.Applying IP address node

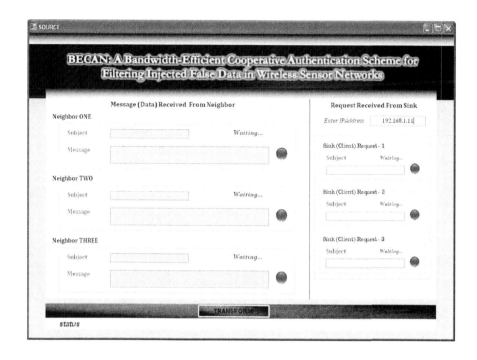

Fig15. Applying message in each node

Fig16. Data transmitting for nodes

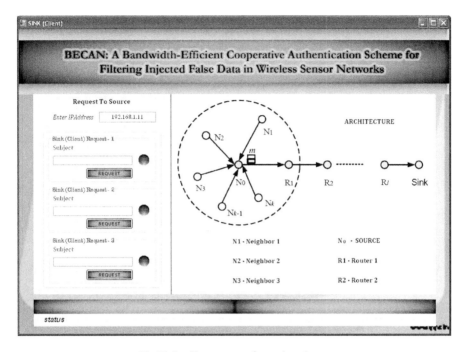

Fig17. Sending message for each node

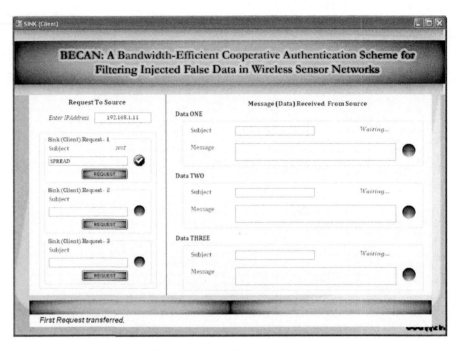

Fig18. Data transmitted to node 1

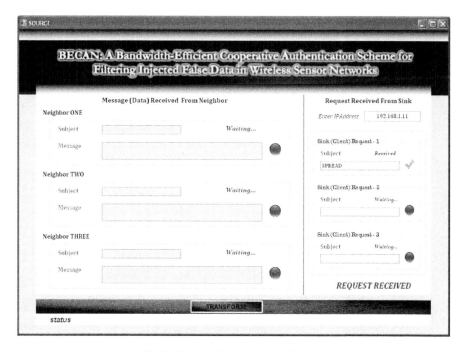

Fig19. Data received by the receiver

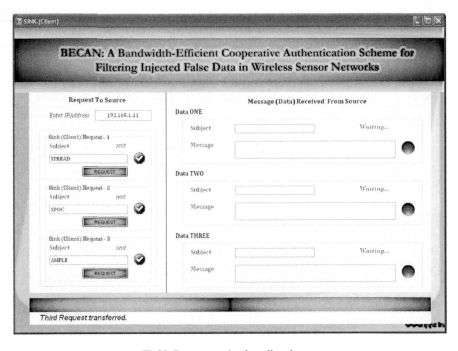

Fig20. Data transmitted to all nodes

SOURCE

BECAN: A Bandwidth-Efficient Cooperative Authentication Scheme for Filtering Injected False Data in Wireless Sensor Networks

| Message (Data) Received From Neighbor | | Request Received From Sink |

Neighbor ONE

Subject _____ *Waiting...*

Message _____

Neighbor TWO

Subject _____ *Waiting...*

Message _____

Neighbor THREE

Subject _____ *Waiting...*

Message _____

Enter IPAddress 192.168.1.11

Sink (Client) Request - 1

Subject   *Received*

SPREAD   ✓

Sink (Client) Request - 2

Subject   *Received*

SPOC   ✓

Sink (Client) Request - 3

Subject   *Received*

AMPLE   ✓

REQUEST RECEIVED

TRANSFORM

status

41

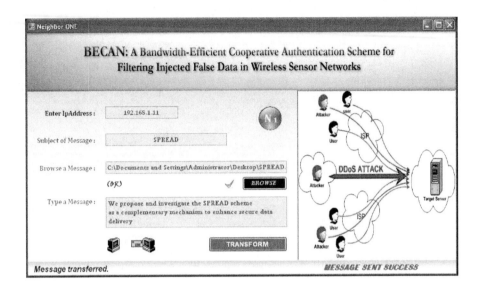

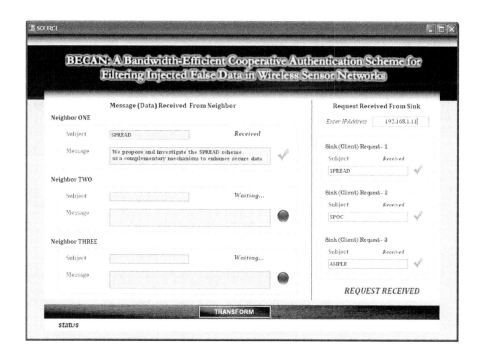

Fig21. Data received all paths

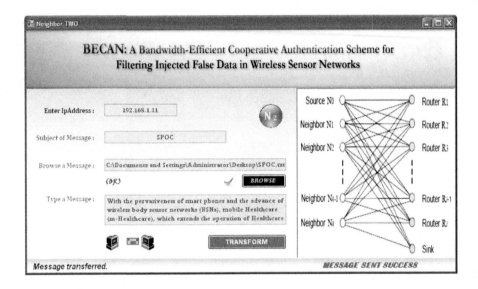

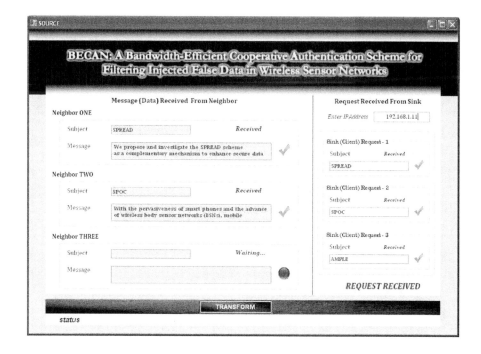

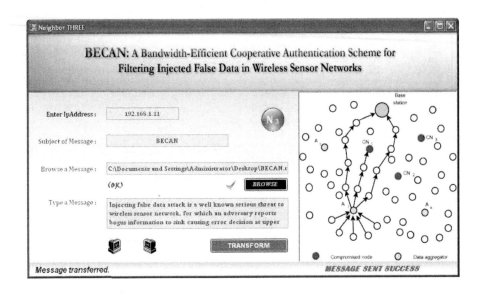

BECAN: A Bandwidth-Efficient Cooperative Authentication Scheme for Filtering Injected False Data in Wireless Sensor Networks

Message (Data) Received From Neighbor

Request Received From Sink

Neighbor ONE

Enter IPAddress 192.168.1.11

Subject   SPREAD   *Received*

Sink (Client) Request - 1

Message   We propose and investigate the SPREAD scheme   ✓
           as a complementary mechanism to enhance secure data

Subject   *Received*

SPREAD   ✓

Neighbor TWO

Subject   SPOC   *Received*

Sink (Client) Request - 2

Subject   *Received*

Message   With the pervasiveness of smart phones and the advance   ✓
           of wireless body sensor networks (BSNs), mobile

SPOC   ✓

Neighbor THREE

Sink (Client) Request - 3

Subject   BECAN   *Received*

Subject   *Received*

AMPLE   ✓

Message   Injecting false data attack is a well-known serious threat   ✓
           to wireless sensor network, for which an adversary

REQUEST RECEIVED

TRANSFORM

status

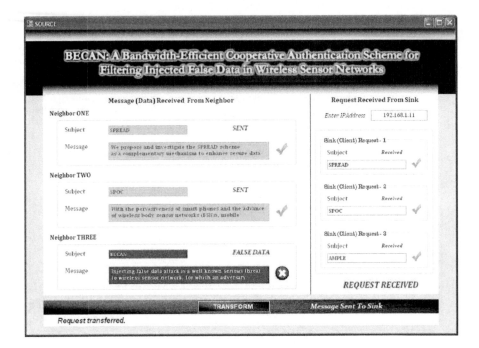

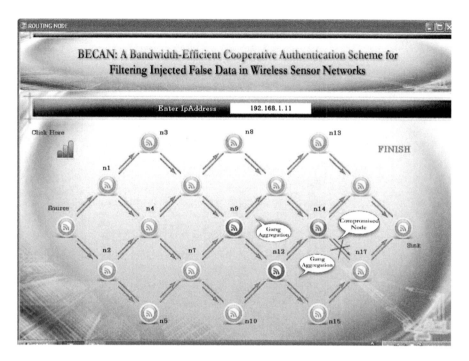

Fig22. Data injected node

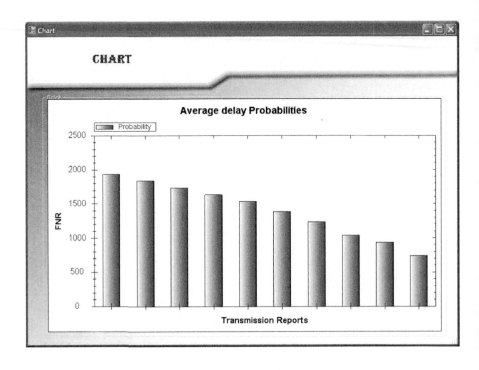

Fig23. Probability range

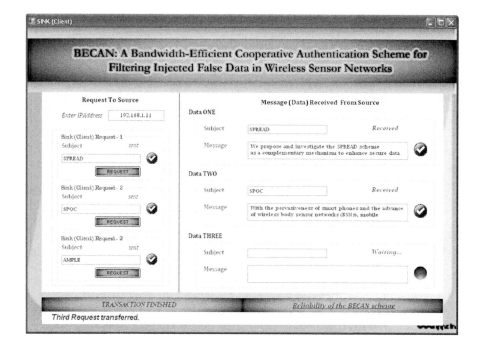

Reliability of the BECAN scheme

$$FNR = \frac{\text{number of true data that cannot reach the } sink}{\text{total number of true data}}$$

$$FNR = \frac{1}{3}$$

REFERENCES

[1] R. Szewczky, A. Mainwaring, J. Anderson, and D. Culler, "An Analysis of a Large Scale Habit Monitoring Application," *Proc. Second ACM Int'l Conf. Embedded Networked Sensor Systems (Sensys '04)*, 2004.

[2] L. Eschenauer and V.D. Gligor, "A Key-Management Scheme for Distributed Sensor Networks," *Proc. Ninth ACM Conf. Computer and Comm. Security (CCS '02)*, 2002.

[3] R. Lu, X. Lin, C. Zhang, H. Zhu, P. Ho, and X. Shen, "AICN: An Efficient Algorithm to Identify Compromised Nodes in Wireless Sensor Network," *Proc. IEEE Int'l Conf. Comm. (ICC '08)*, May 2008.

[4] X. Lin, R. Lu, and X. Shen, "MDPA: Multidimensional Privacy-Preserving Aggregation Scheme for Wireless Sensor Networks," *Wireless Comm. and Mobile Computing*, vol. 10, pp. 843-856, 2010.

[5] X. Lin, "CAT: Building Couples to Early Detect Node Compromise Attack in Wireless Sensor Networks," *Proc. IEEE GLOBECOM '09*, Nov.-Dec. 2009.

[6] K. Ren, W. Lou, and Y. Zhang, "Multi-User Broadcast Authentication in Wireless Sensor Networks," *Proc. IEEE Sensor Ad Hoc Comm. Networks (SECON '07)*, June 2007.

[7] L. Zhou and C. Ravishankar, "A Fault Localized Scheme for False Report Filtering in Sensor Networks," *Proc. Int'l Conf. Pervasive Services, (ICPS '05)*, pp. 59-68, July 2005.

[8] Z. Zhu, Q. Tan, and P. Zhu, "An Effective Secure Routing for False Data Injection Attack in Wireless Sensor Network," *Proc. 10th Asia-Pacific Network Operations and Management Symp. (APNOMS '07)*, pp. 457-465, 2007.

[9] F. Ye, H. Luo, S. Lu, and L. Zhang, "Statistical En-Route Detection and Filtering of Injected False Data in Sensor Networks," *Proc. IEEE INFOCOM '04*, Mar. 2004.

[10] S. Zhu, S. Setia, S. Jajodia, and P. Ning, "An Interleaved Hop-by-Hop Authentication Scheme for Filtering of Injected False Data in Sensor Networks," *Proc. IEEE Symp. Security and Privacy*, 2004.

[11] H. Yang, F. Ye, Y. Yuan, S. Lu, and W. Arbaugh, "Toward Resilient Security in Wireless Sensor Networks," *Proc. Sixth ACM Int'l Symp. Mobile Ad Hoc Networking and Computing (MobiHoc '05)*, pp. 34-45, 2005.

[12] K. Ren, W. Lou, and Y. Zhang, "LEDS: Providing Location-Aware End-to-End Data Security in Wireless Sensor Networks," *Proc. IEEE INFOCOM '06*, Apr. 2006.

[13] Y. Zhang, W. Liu, W. Lou, and Y. Fang, "Location-Based Compromise-Tolerant Security

Mechanisms for Wireless Sensor Networks," *IEEE J. Selected Areas in Comm.*, vol. 24, no. 2, pp. 247-260, Feb. 2006.

[14] C.-M. Yu, C.-S. Lu, and S.-Y. Kuo, "A Dos-Resilient En-Route Filtering Scheme for Sensor Networks," *Proc. Tenth ACM Int'l Symp. Mobile Ad Hoc Networking and Computing (MobiHoc '09),* pp. 343-344, 2009.

[15] J. Chen, Q. Yu, Y. Zhang, H.-H. Chen, and Y. Sun, "Feedback Based Clock Synchronization in Wireless Sensor Networks: A Control Theoretic Approach," *IEEE Trans. Vehicular Technology,* vol. 59, no. 6, pp. 2963-2973, June 2010.[16] S. He, J. Chen, Y. Sun, D.K.Y. Yau, and N.K. Yip, "On Optimal Information Capture by Energy-Constrained Mobile Sensors,"*IEEE Trans. Vehicular Technology,* vol. 59, no. 5, pp. 2472-2484, June 2010.

[17] K. Akkaya and M. Younis, "A Survey on Routing Protocols for Wireless Sensor Networks," *Ad Hoc Networks,* vol. 3, no. 3, pp. 325-349, May 2005.

[18] V.C. Giruka, M. Singhal, J. Royalty, and S. Varanasi, "Security in Wireless Sensor Networks," *Wireless Comm. and Mobile Computing,* vol. 8, no. 1, pp. 1-24, Jan. 2008.

[19] A. Liu and P. Ning, "TinyECC: A Configurable Library for Elliptic Curve Cryptography in Wireless Sensor Networks," *Proc. Seventh Int'l Conf. Information Processing in Sensor Networks (IPSN '08),* pp. 245-256, Apr. 2008.

[20] J. Dong, Q. Chen, and Z. Niu, "Random Graph Theory Based Connectivity Analysis in Wireless Sensor Networks with Rayleigh Fading Channels," *Proc. Asia-Pacific Conf. Comm. (APCC '07),* pp. 123-126, Oct. 2007.

[21] MICAz: Wireless Measurement
System, http://www.xbow.com/Products/Product_pdf_files/Wireless_pdfMICAz_Data sheet.pdf, 2010.

[22] Imote2: High-Performance Wireless Sensor Network
Node, http://www.xbow.com/Products/Product_pdf_files/_Wireless_pdfImote2_Dat asheet.pdf, 2010.

[23] C. Boyd, W. Mao, and K.G. Paterson, "Key Agreement Using Statically Keyed Authenticators," *Proc. Second Int'l Conf. Applied Cryptography and Network Security ˉC (ACNS '04),* pp. 248-262, 2004.

[24] J. Black and P. Rogaway, "Cbc Macs for Arbitrary-Length Messages: the Three-Key Constructions," *J. Cryptology,* vol. 18, no. 2, pp. 111-131, 2005.

[25] W. Mao, *Modern Cryptography: Theory and Practice.* Prentice Hall PTR, 2003.

[26] X. Li, N. Santoro, and I. Stojmenovic, "Localized Distance-Sensitive Service Discovery in

Wireless Sensor and Actor Networks,"*IEEE Trans. Computers,* vol. 58, no. 9, pp. 1275-1288, Sept. 2009.

[27] X. Li, A. Nayak, D. Simplot-Ryl, and I. Stojmenovic, "Sensor Placement in Sensor and Actuator Networks," *Wireless Sensor and Actuator Networks: Algorithms and Protocols for Scalable Coordination and Data Communication,* Wiley, 2010.

[28] X. Du, Y. Xiao, M. Guizani, and H.-H. Chen, "An Effective Key Management Scheme for Heterogeneous Sensor Networks," *Ad Hoc Networks,* vol. 5, pp. 24-34, Jan. 2007.

[29] R. Canetti, J. Garay, G. Itkis, D. Micciancio, M. Naor, and B. Pinkas, "Multicast Security: A Taxonomy and Some Efficient Constructions," *Proc. IEEE INFOCOM '99,* pp. 708-716, Mar. 1999.

[30] Z. Benenson, C. Freiling, E. Hammerschmidt, S. Lucks, and L. Pimenidis, "Authenticated Query Flooding in Sensor Networks,"*Security and Privacy in Dynamic Environments,* Springer, pp. 38-49, July 2006.

[31] X. Lin, R. Lu, P. Ho, X. Shen, and Z. Cao, "TUA: A Novel Compromise-Resilient Authentication Architecture for Wireless Mesh Networks," *IEEE Trans. Wireless Comm.,* vol. 7, no. 4, pp. 1389-1399, Apr. 2008.

[32] C. Zhang, R. Lu, X. Lin, P. Ho, and X. Shen, "An Efficient Identity-Based Batch Verification Scheme for Vehicular Sensor Networks," *Proc. IEEE INFOCOM '08,* Apr. 2008.

Printed in Great Britain
by Amazon

87556728R00037

Nia Lloyd

SpringerWienNewYork

Niels Peter Rygaard

Severe Attachment Disorder
in Childhood

A Guide to Practical Therapy

SpringerWienNewYork

Dr. Niels Peter Rygaard
Clin. Psychologist, authorized by D.P.A., Aarhus C, Denmark

Translated from
N. P. Rygaard, L'enfant abandonné.
Guide de traitement des troubles de l'attachement.
© De Boeck & Larcier s.a., 2005, 1e édition
Editions De Boeck Université, Rue des Minimes 39, 1000 Bruxelles, Belgium

© 2006 Springer-Verlag/Wien
Printed in Austria
SpringerWienNewYork is a part of
Springer Science + Business Media
springer.com

Printing: Druckerei Theiss GmbH, 9431 St. Stefan, Austria
Printed on acid-free and chlorine-free bleached paper
SPIN: 11571957

With 3 Figures

Library of Congress Control Number: 2006924573

ISBN-10 3-211-29705-7 SpringerWienNewYork
ISBN-13 978-3-211-29705-6 SpringerWienNewYork

CONTENTS

General introduction

PART I
A.D. DEVELOPMENT FROM CONCEPTION TO ADULTHOOD

Chapter 1
Causes and symptoms

Chapter 2
Stages in self-organization

Chapter 6
Arrested emotional personality development

PART II
THERAPY

Chapter 7
How can you practice milieu therapy?

Chapter 8
Milieu therapy during pregnancy, birth to age 3

Transient bonding problems and attachment disorder in adopted children

Chapter 9
Milieu therapy for the preschool child

Chapter 12
Milieu therapy for the juvenile

Chapter 13
Attachment disorder, sexual behavior problems and sexual abuse

PART III
GUIDELINES FOR ORGANIZING THE THERAPEUTIC MILIEU

Chapter 14
The personal development of the AD caretaker

Chapter 15
Developing the professional AD team

Chapter 16
Methods for the AD teamwork

GENERAL INTRODUCTION

Society has not yet been very successful in finding ways to prevent Attachment Disorder (hereafter: AD) in general or in developing successful therapeutic methods for the individual child. If the first relationships in life have gone wrong, they seem to be very difficult to remedy later in life. Attachment seems to be a "window", wide open from birth and gradually closing more or less towards age 3.

My hope is to give the reader a realistic approach to the problem, and to lay out a broad range of theoretical and practical pathways in this challenging field.

Please note the distinction that this text is devoted to cases of *severe* Attachment Disorder: the subject is *not* children who have only experienced single traumatic life events – they have a much better prognosis – it concerns children who have survived multiple traumatic events, perhaps also hunger, and a persistent lack of coherent parenting in their first years. Also, the therapeutic frameworks and understandings in this book can be understood as *tools providing a very secure base for the child.* Emotional security is a must for almost all other lines of development. If the secure environment is provided, some children who seem at first glance to be "rather hopeless cases" will start developing at a faster rate after a year or two. Others with a more genuine handicap will also function better, but may need the secure environment for many years.

It is also important to understand that these children are normal children whose abnormal behavior is caused by an abnormal early environment.

In this book a lot of effort has been put into making AD behavior comprehensible and de-mystified. This is because you cannot solve a problem, unless you profoundly understand the nature of it – and AD problems have a tendency to distort our sense of proportion. A lot of everyday examples are used to illustrate symptoms, theory and practice.

If I have succeeded, the contents should not be difficult to understand, whereas working with the AD child in practice is a constant challenge to your convictions and responsibility. It is a guide trying to answer some of the common questions puzzling people working with children and juveniles suffering from Attachment Disorder:

– Why is there an increasing number of AD children?
– What are the causes of an AD development in children?
– How does AD show in behavior and personality?
– How do you practice treatment or therapy at different develop-ment stages during childhood?
– What can you do to prevent an AD development, or to reduce the symptoms and consequences?
– What happens to people, groups and organizations working with these children?
– How do you develop and maintain your therapeutic attitude and the structure of treatment?

First, let me give you a short introduction to the problem of AD in general.

What is "attachment"?

In brief, the theory of attachment was developed from 1950 and onwards by John Bowlby (1969, 1973, 1988). Bowlby suggested early attachment (0–3 years) as an inborn behavior program in primates and especially humans. Bowlby's main idea was that the attachment behavioral system had evolved to increase the likelihood of the infant's protection and survival. This protection is mainly based on physical closeness and contact between mother and baby in the first few years. If proximity is disturbed or hindered, a number of characteristic behaviors appear in both parent and baby, such as crying, searching for the other, mourning, etc.

The system is thus activated by separation, and seems to be stabilized already at age one.

In "The Strange Situation Test", Mary Ainsworth (1978) detected three characteristic reaction patterns (or strategies for proximity) when the mother left the room, and later a fourth pattern was detected. During this simple and ingeniously designed test, the mother and the 1-year old child are introduced to a lab room with interesting toys, the mother leaves the room for two times three minutes during the test, and the child's reaction at separation and reunion is observed. These patterns seen at age one persist into adulthood for 70% of the children, and they seem to be passed on from one generation to the next by the caretaker's attachment behavior.

The four patterns are:

• **Secure/autonomous**

The child reacts when the mother leaves, but explores the room after a while, seeks contact with the mother again and is soothed, and quickly starts exploring the room again. There is closeness and mutual joy in contact between mother and baby.

• **Avoidant**

The child apparently does not react to the absence of the mother and is consumed with handling the objects in the room. The mother when returning also directs her interests towards objects rather than the child. Studies demonstrate that the child is in fact very stressed by the absence and that this stress persists longer than in the secure child. The child seems to know that showing the appropriate feelings of separation may lead to rejection, and therefore controls the expression of these feelings. A lot of energy is used to suppress the natural attachment reactions.

• **Ambivalent**

The child clings to the mother and can at the same time show anger or controlling behaviour even before the mother leaves the room. The child does not explore the room but is preoccupied with the mother's absence, and does not resume playing activity after the return of the mother. It seems to try to reassure itself of a proximity of which it is insecure. The attachment system is so to speak hyper-activated, leaving no room for the fulfilment of other needs.

• **Disorganized/disoriented**

The child's behaviour contains elements from one of the previous patterns, but the child doesn't respond to separation and reunion in any coherent pattern. It may "freeze" in a stiffened position, throw itself on the floor, cling to the mother and at the same time turn the face away from her, etc. This pattern has been found to be related with later personality disturbances and other problems. Approximately 15% of all 1 year old children display the disorganized pattern. Some (but not all) of these children later develop attachment disorder.

It is remarkable that only the secure/autonomous attachment allows the child to explore and engage itself in the environment most of the time. The three alternative patterns consume the child's attention and energy so much, that exploration and development is put aside in the attempt to recreate the secure base. As said by the Greek philosopher Archimedes: "Give me a place to stand, and I will move the Earth". A secure first relationship is the standpoint and prerequisite for experiencing life and development.

The problems of disorganized contact are the main concern of this book. This very short description of general attachment patterns is only to mention the tradition that embeds the concept of attachment disorder. For the reader interested in a deeper theoretical understanding of the concepts of attachment theory, Shaver and Cassidy's (1999) excellent handbook is inevitable.

What is "attachment disorder"?

There is a fundamental problem in writing this book: the concept of normal attachment is being extensively researched, but "Attachment Disorder" is not a clearly defined, agreed-upon diagnostic entity. It is much discussed, and there are not enough scientific studies to define it clearly. There is a growing number of studies mapping normal attachment patterns in both children and couple relationships, but abnormal attachment patterns have received little scientific interest and funding. Only major catastrophic events (such as World War II) have produced a large number of abandoned children with attachment problems, and subsequently have spurred a period of research in AD. Studies tend to bulk unevenly in periods where AD problems are frequent in society.

This documentation problem leaves parents and practitioners in a void: what to do with severely disturbed children here and now? Disturbed children are indeed very real and call for immediate action every day. In order to overcome this gap between theory and practice I have described these problems through case stories, and I have provided some attitudes and tools for the caretakers which have proven valuable in everyday practice to some extent. Also, studies from different fields have been included in understanding. The title of *severe* Attachment Disorder is intended to limit the text to children who have been so deprived or stressed in early life that they can't be reached by more traditional methods, such as psychotherapy.

The hallmark of attachment disordered children is a much reduced ability to respond adequately emotionally and socially. In the very short version Attachment Disorder (hence: AD) covers a range of behavior problems that are common in children who did not receive sufficient care during the first few years. As we shall see, the problem of AD is a complex one, but in headlines the most important criteria will suffice:

A. Antisocial behavior throughout childhood

Intimidating, impulsive, violent and aggressive behavior, low ability to learn from social experiences (including punishment/restrictions). The child may have a sadistic or socially destructive intent, hurt other children or animals, display a lack of lasting shame, guilt and remorse, blaming only others when confronted. Fight/flight/freeze behavior (vagabonding, endless conflicts, stubbornness) is typical.

B. Uncritical attachment behavior

The child will be charming and "trustful" towards new persons and case managers at random. The child is unable to distinguish emotionally between familiar and non-familiar persons, is often clinging ("like tape"). The child displays immature attachment behavior (has the contact behavior pattern normal at age 6–12 months). The child has short and superficial contact patterns. A lasting relationship will not result from these random contacts.

The diagnosis has the premise that deprivation, neglect or abuse has been a major element of early childhood, and it can't be made with any certainty before the child is about seven years old.

There are many individual variations of these basic patterns of disturbed attachment, such as the very introvert, secluded and self-destructive children who are equally unable to function in social relationships, and at the other end of the scale very extrovert, impulsive/aggressive children.

The main issue is that the child will be much disabled when trying to develop a mutual, loving, obliging relationship to others. The social competences being compromised, other aspects of life – such as playing, learning, working, mating, being a family or group member will suffer as well. Negative reactions from others (conflicts and disappointment) will disturb daily development. Therefore, the intellectual learning capacities will not be put sufficiently to use and many of these children develop secondary problems such as a lack of learning, criminal activity and drug abuse.

In the specific child multiple early strains and trauma may add other problems to life. Often AD is seen in combination with:

- Post Traumatic Stress Disorder (PTSD), a state of chronic stress due to single extremely traumatic events.
- Attention Deficit, Hyperactive Disorder (ADHD), extrovert and disorganized behavior due to organic nervous system problems.
- Post-Institutional Autistic Syndrome (PIAS), a state of passive and introvert "frozenness" due to neglect.
- Tourette's syndrome, the child suffers from multiple motor and vocal tics for more than a year. In rare cases the involuntary use of obscene words is also seen. May be accompanied by obsessive-compulsive disorder and ADHD. The disease is probably genetically determined.

Only a clinical examination of the child in question can map how other problems interfere with a disturbed early attachment. Unfortunately the possibilities of such examinations are scarce in most places.

The diagnosis of AD and its predecessors has been much discussed and challenged. In particular because professionals of course hesitate to use such a severe diagnosis early in life, and because far too radical methods (developed in desperation of these children's emotional inaccessibility) have been associated with the diagnosis. Such as "holding therapy" where the child is immobilized by adults for hours, trying to make the child accept the authority and love of foster parents or adoptive parents. In one case, a child has died from asphyxiation as a result of holding "therapy". This of course has made the diagnosis even more controversial.

I shall try to give the reader a balanced view of the problem, as well as a number of methods that are reasonable and practical. Meanwhile, science will hopefully produce more extensive documentation and methods for treatment.

How does attachment disorder come about in general? I shall describe my personal view of the problem. You should be aware that this introduction is my personal view of the actual problems of attachment in society, and not a scientifically based review.

Early attachment: a worldwide challenge

We spent several million years in refining the early mother/child relationship – and a mere 15 years in breaking it down. From World War II and onwards – accelerating about 1960 – we started the largest social experiment ever undertaken in the western world – mothers of preschool children and babies went to work outside their homes, away from their infants. This not only changed our whole culture: religious beliefs, family patterns, traditions, eating habits, number of children in a family, family income, but it also broke up the mother and child relationship into a whole new way of being attached. The conditions for learning how to become human through early childhood relationships were turned upside down. Today, we are probably the only species of mammals where mother and baby do not stay together inseparable for at least the first two to three years after birth. Ask the gorillas or the blue whales, they will shake their heads in wonder.

In my country, Denmark, it only took fifteen years (1960–75) to sweep 80% of all women out of their homes in the daytime, and into factories and offices. The great stabilizers of society – the working class culture and the country life culture – disappeared almost overnight. The cultural pivot – the family – was split up into members-meeting-between-other-activities. As a first radical change, the number of children being born at home and not in a hospital or a clinic fell from 85% in 1955 to less than 1% in 1975. The first physical contact for the baby was no longer an autonomous decision of parental judgment, but a staff decision, with the parents as spectators, sometimes from behind a glass wall.

To say the least, staff decisions were not always wise, and today many adults suffer from the consequences of early separation. And so do their mothers. Enforced early separation not only produces disturbed infants, but also disturbed parents. Mothers who are physically separated from their newborns – even for very short whiles – often experience lasting intense, irrational feelings of guilt, tend to feel detached and alienated towards the baby, and feel incompetent and insecure trying to interpret the baby's signals and needs, and they become insecure when deciding how to act towards the baby. This of course will often provoke a reciprocal loop of misunderstanding and unfulfilled needs between mother and baby. Not to mention how a father, excluded from the birth experience and physical contact with the baby, should initiate any devotion to a baby arriving from hospital long after birth, deprived of the possibility of physical bonding with his child.

The next result of the changes in working patterns, and delayed some 5 years (parallel to women leaving home for work) were the exploding number of divorces, producing a new role in Danish families: the unprotected and overworked single mother. In many ways, this development became a disruption of a lot of families rather than the exciting lifestyle renewal and adequate re-orientation it was meant to be. The material wealth produced by the both-parents-at-work family produces reproductive poverty: today, the European population is 25% of global population, in 20 years it will be a mere 17%.

And finally (if you are still with me), the grandparents disappeared from the home, taking with them all their irritating traditional knowledge of how to cope with 8 children, incessant births, child disease and good cooking, leaving behind their bewildered offspring to become parents as best they could. Consultants, baby magazines and other substitutes partly replaced them.

Today's average parents are relatively old when the first baby arrives. They never had to be responsible for baby sisters and brothers, they met a lot of new people early on in life, they didn't see their parents or grandparents much, and when they hold their firstborn in their arms, they don't know a thing about what to do – except being extremely ambitious on their own and on the child's behalf!

The problems children have in personality development have changed. The neurotic personality (deeply attached, but caught in the age 3–5 conflict between self-realization and a strict superego) also disappeared with the changes in family structure and moral codes, and was replaced by the intelligent, spoiled, emotionally insecure child, without a few solid role models, prone to following it's own mind and to be unaffected by authorities. Later to become ludomanic, narcissistic, running for 6 hours a day, or just plain exhausted by exaggerated ambition and illusions of eternal youth.

Child psychology theory has been hesitant in adjusting to this change. In fact, our treatment philosophy, methods (such as play therapy and talking therapies) and general ideas about what children need, is still mostly directed towards neurosis problems. And sadly so, these methods in my experience are often downright anti-therapeutic when addressing the small number of children with severe AD problems. We emphasize that children should take their own decisions and social initiatives and work in changing groups during the day. This is adequate for the great majority of children who have parental back-up, but much too difficult for children who carry little basic trust with them from home.

Today, 80% of all Danish children age 6–36 months spend most of their waking hours in a day care or in a kindergarten. In 1948 Denmark, children's work contributed with 25% to the average family income. Now, children have become an expense, a problem and also a luxury – that's why we have so few, and so late in life. Today the infant must from an early age face a more or less predictable number of adults and other children, who often are interchanged kaleidoscopically during the day. One important quality of the secure/autonomous parent is accessibility, and I may wonder how many infants experience accessibility in relationships to their professional caretakers.

Science tells us that a newborn, with any luck, can attach to 4–5 persons before the age of 3, and still turn out as a normal, healthy adult. The daycare is very successful in supplementing the parental efforts (probably because it resembles the family setting), whereas one might be worried about the very small children who spend long days in an institution with many other children and only a few professionals. The NICHD daycare study (2003) found daycare to be a healthy way of caring for children, however those under two years who spend many hours in daycare tend to develop more behavioral problems. Although the study is not detailed enough to point out the exact reasons, it gives reason to worry about how much separation from the parent small children can endure. Also the former socialist countries where the state used to provide free nursing while mother was at work now face the problem that many parents can't afford qualified care for their child, while many of them have both two or three jobs just in order to survive.

One of the most expensive goods in today's society is a professional caretaker for the many hours where both parents are at work. This price increases compared to other household expenses because childcare cannot be rationalized or computerized as so many other functions in society – it is based on personal contact.

I am certainly not talking about the "good old days" concerning early childcare –perhaps children in the Western World never had better conditions, and child mortality was never lower than at present. Today we have a society based on women's full participation in working society – and therefore it must be the duty of society to support the family and especially the mother for the first few years. Through a prolonged leave after birth, ample and cheap opportunities for secure care for the baby/toddler when parents are at work, and free extra education and updating when the mother returns to her job after the leave. This is a small price for society to pay, considering how much wealth women's work contributes to the economic growth in society. Even more so, this is necessary in the countries where industrialization is developing very fast, and mothers have extremely long working hours while being paid next to nothing.

How many children lost a secure attachment in the process of the sudden change in the premises of early bonding? Still using Denmark as an example, there is a system where every new mother has several free visits from a district health nurse from birth until the child is aged 3. These nurses stated (1992) that in general 80% of all infants are feeling psychologically safe and thrive well – they can cope with the many early contacts because of a stable relationship to relatively harmonious parents. So, for society in general, we haven't reached the panic level – yet. But, and that is serious enough, 15% have minor signs of deprivation, such as malnutrition (obesity, skinny, vitamin deprivation), and signs of feeling too insecure to spend their time learning in something they could perceive as a safe environment. They have experienced too many divorces, institutions, and shifting persons to make life a happy experience. In spite of a soaring rise in school expenses, all paid by the state, 1/3 of all children who are leaving school describe themselves as losers in the system, and have a generally low self-esteem. From 1985 to 1999, special school classes for children in Denmark with socio-emotional problems have in-creased 300%, according to the state office of statistics, whereas the number of other special need classes has been stable (Amtsraads-foreningen 2000).

5% of all Danish infants show clear signs of extensive deprivation, seriously lack contact ability, suffer from the psychological conse-quences of violence, sexual abuse, malnutrition, etc. These children practically always grow up with a retarded emotional development, and are often suffering from an array of severe personality disorders or psychosis.

We might have absorbed and adjusted better to this change in patterns of raising children, had it not happened so fast. Disrupted bonding is probably not resulting only from the nature of social changes (children in some old cultures are successfully raised in groups), but from the very speed of change, preventing the gradual adaptation to new life conditions.

Let me exemplify this idea by describing the experiences of the English anthropologist Turnbull (1987): He lived with the Ik-tribe in the highlands of Uganda and found a people who stole from each other, who ignored the elderly and the children, who apparently considered cheating and deceit to be an art form. He only found one single girl who made any attempt to attach, but the parents incarcerated her considering this behavior to be highly abnormal. Eventually she died, and the parents threw the carcass out to the animals. In general, children from the age of 3 grew up in gangs without role models, and from the age of 2 were stealing food in order to survive. Well, you might say, this is somewhere far away, but Turnbull wanted to know why this culture had so many AD members. He studied their history and found that 40 years earlier this had been a much larger, kinder and very social people of hunters and gatherers. Overnight they had been deprived of their hunting grounds by the government, and with no time to adjust to a new environment in the mountains which were formerly only a temporary resting place, the culture as a whole had deteriorated.

Another case: In Greenland, the Eskimo tribes had for thousands of years adjusted to a life in small hunting communities along the coast. They had rich traditions for infant care and upbringing. Among these were that in spring the whole tribe made a three-day picnic in the mountains where those born in winter would exercise how to walk, and all attempts to stagger along were celebrated by the members of the tribe. Around 1960, the Danish Government, by "persuasion," moved almost all natives into newly built towns. 15 years later, the next generation suffered from an enormous percentage of maladjusted, alcoholic, psychotic and identity-bereaved youngsters, with a soaring ratio of suicides. Even today, suicide is frequent in Greenland youth. The American Indians share a similar fate.

The breakdown of Communism and of society in general in Russia, Rumania and other countries has produced a host of abandoned children surviving in street gangs, and of adopted children who are frustrating countless adoptive parents who had expected that love would heal any wound, and who as a consequence have been hurt themselves. I remember a lunch break at my work in 1988 where one of the staff members uttered: "Let's build a new wing for Romanian children from adoptive families" – sadly, his doomsday vision proved largely correct. Hoksbergen (2004) has made extensive studies of foreign children adopted into Holland, especially a study of 74 Romanian adopted children. His estimate after follow-ups and testing is that half of the children suffer from severe AD.

At the other extreme of the change/tradition scale we find societies that have abandoned development in favor of stability and a tight network, such as the Amish of North America who with a stable lifestyle have practically no overtly AD or otherwise seriously personality disturbed members. Even those psychopaths, who according to the laws of statistics should be present, seem to be encapsulated by the overlying traditions and strong uniform social codes of everyday life.

These examples go to illustrate the idea that any very fast change in society can overrule the adaptation capacity of many families and individuals, and in some cases will result – in the next generation – in some easily recognizable physical symptoms and personality disturbances. The gap between those who adapt – thanks to stable parental care – and those who do not, is widening.

What happens when they grow up?

Statistics indicate that some 15 to 20 years after the abovementioned radical change in the Danish mother's workplace – when the babies exposed to early random contact with persons other than the parents reached youth – the following juvenile problems accelerated intensely:

- Personality Disorders (Antisocial Personality, Borderline).
- Severe Identity Problems, feelings of meaninglessness and lack of lust for life.
- Depressive states and suicide attempts (Denmark, in spite of equalized wealth and extensive social care has one of the highest suicide rates in the world – especially accelerating for young girls).
- Self-infliction, withdrawal or aggressive or stereotype, meaningless behavior.
- Addiction Problems.
- Altered activity levels (hyper-and hypo activity).
- Eating Disorders (anorexia nervosa, bulimia).
- Autoimmune diseases (such as certain forms of rash, arthritis and asthma)

These symptoms have always been part of the puberty crisis – but now, more youngsters cross that line and reach a regular state of dysfunction and are in dire need of treatment.

Exactly the above-mentioned youth disorders have one striking feature in common – they are similar to the reactions of babies separated for too long from their mothers!

Could it be that those who have had discrete symptoms of bereavement as infants repeat these symptoms more intensely in the next life growth period – puberty? And that this crisis, instead of leading to a transformation into adulthood, leads to a domino-effect imbalance and subsequent regression? I think so – this is of course

PART I

A.D. DEVELOPMENT FROM CONCEPTION TO ADULTHOOD

Causes and symptoms

A systemic perspective of the relationship between mother and child

Contact, self-organization and the development of constancy

Consequences of contact disruption

My love is like some raven
at my window with a broken wing.

Bob Dylan (From "Love Minus Zero")

other. From the moment of conception (contact between two genetic information codes), to physical attachment (contact between embryo and womb), through pregnancy (contact between fetus and womb through the umbilical cord), birth (from constant physical contact by skin and breast to intermittent contact), to sensory contact (the child learns to recognize sensory patterns through daily routines and maternal attention), sensory-motor contact (the child learns to organize its responses to attention, reflexes mature into intentional behavior and experiences with action/reaction circuits), to psychological contact (development of attachment and creation of an internal conception of the mother, still more independent of her physical presence), to social contact (development of self-recognition, learning social contact patterns, solving internal conflicts of personal needs versus social demands, learning the family roles and achieving self-conscience).

The natural development of contact seems to move gradually from uninterrupted physical contact and external dependency to contact with oneself (internal communication between emotions, attention, thoughts, memory, language, behavior patterns), and thereby the child obtains a relative independency of the immediate surroundings. At the age of two, the normal child is fundamentally able to discriminate and choose what and whom to contact, physically and psychologically. Eat some things and not other things, take an interest in some toys and not in others, contact some people and avoid others, to miss an absent person or to look forward to her presence.

Also, contact seems to move from a symbiotic state through an antagonistic and conflicting state helping the child to separate and to establish physical and psychological boundaries, ending in a separated and stabilized state of mind and emotion. Without initial contact, a child cannot separate and function independently, and a lack of initial contact is a characteristic of the later AD child. It remains utterly dependent on the immediate surroundings and on constant, strong feedback from others: internal functions have not been solidly established; therefore external help is necessary much longer than in the life of a secure child.

The organization of the self

The word "organ" is Greek, meaning "tool". In this text, self-organization is the child's genetically determined internal tendency to develop emotions, behavior patterns and faculties, internal self-regulating systems that gradually turn from dependency of external stimulation to internal regulation and self-adjustment. This "tool-making" requires an internal division of labor, such as cells functionally specializing in the embryo, or the two brain hemispheres specializing when processing information.

The very purpose of raising children is to translate a faculty into some behavior the child can apprehend, and repeating it under different circumstances until the child has organized a similar internal function.

Learning how to read is a good example: you translate your ability into a behavior directed towards the child. The child starts by imitating your body posture and words when you read, and it gradually grasps the pattern of transforming something seen into something articulated. It has established an internal coding pattern, and is able to read without your attention and support. Together you have built a self-organizing reading function in the child. The same cycles appear in learning how to eat, drink, move, laugh, love, play, socialize, and so on.

The development of constancy

Compared to the adult, the child can be characterized in one word: instability. The term "constancy" (from Latin, "to stand with") is used by psychologists to describe the degree of internal stability (despite external changes) developed in different areas of development. One important form is called *object constancy*: the child is gradually able to recognize and remember the mother (the object of attention), it develops an inner representation of her, which in time becomes independent of her physical presence. Old people who had a lot of early interaction with mother will still talk about her with affection – although she may have been dead for decades, strong emotional memories of her still guide their actions and form the working model of all later relationships.

Constancy can be defined as: The ability to uphold a function on changing external backgrounds.

E.g.: You ask a 2-year-old child to fetch a cup in the kitchen. On its way the child is disturbed by a lot of interesting objects; maybe someone talks to it about something else. How much diversion can the child cope with, and still remember the cup in the kitchen and return with it? Or you hide behind a door and let the baby find you – it is beginning to have a constant idea about your existence or does it start crying the minute your face disappears? If you ask a 4-year-old to fetch a cup, it will probably be able to remember in spite of all diversions on the way out and back.

We should remember that constancy is upheld in spite of our perpetual processing of new information. Just as the matter of our apparently solid body is completely replaced in a lifetime through metabolism with no loss of identity (thanks to genetic code), the random information stream from our surroundings will be ordered in specific patterns through constancy (a psychological code). Constancy is a pattern incessantly struggling to repeat it self, resisting new events and stressing impacts from the surroundings. Even a simple coli bacterium will display an inborn tendency towards constancy: if a gene for insulin production is artificially inserted into the DNA of the coli, the bacteria will obediently start to produce insulin – but after a while, it will dispose of the inserted DNA code piece and return to being a good old ordinary coli bacterium! That is constancy for you! You can say that the constancy mechanism is the core of our identity (Latin: "idens" = to be the same).

The cell wall itself is a semi-permeable membrane, designed to uphold internal constancy, allowing for controlled interaction with the environment. This is the first constancy function of a human being, the embryonic cell establishing internal constancy and yet allowing for contact when adhering to the womb.

Internal constancy in the child probably depends on initial external constancy: the immediate surroundings must have some degree of stability, pattern and predictability, before the child can adapt to changes and create a separate, independent internal pattern of its own. Random response will cause a random internal function. E.g, if the mother does not stimulate the baby regularly, it will have trouble in maintaining a constant body temperature, a constant heartbeat and a steady breathing function. Later in life it will not learn to be aware of an object for very long periods.

CHAPTER 2

STAGES IN SELF-ORGANIZATION

Stages in self-organization

Which internal functional systems are crucial to development? And considering the therapeutic efforts, two questions are vital:

A. What are the most elementary functions that the child has not yet been able to stabilize – where does the degree of constancy not suffice?
B. How can we establish a therapeutic setting where the child can organize these functions into a system, a meaningful whole?

To examine these questions, we may define five early stages of internalizing different functions at different levels, covering the period from the onset of pregnancy to the age of 5. Each is the foundation for the next. Later, disrupting circumstances will be identified at each stage.

Stage I: physical self-organization

The genetic conception process, life in the womb and the birth process form the success of physical organization, in this text especially the organization of the nervous system. The outcome of a normal physical development is a fetus beginning to react to stimuli during pregnancy, able to integrate, mold and respond to stimulation at the end of pregnancy and immediately after birth. A normal nervous system will also tend to seek and establish contact with a mother or any figure that is roughly similar to the mother after birth. The newborn has a capacity for communicating; it can receive and primitively perceive (grade and sort sensory information), and respond.

The result of physical development may be called *organic constancy*: helped by regular stimulation, the child gradually learns to stabilize physical patterns: brain waves, wake and sleep, arousal level, attention, breath, digestion, heart rate, body temperature, reaction to stimulation, defense mechanisms towards infections.

> How can we create an environment that encourages the mother to give the fetus optimal physical conditions during pregnancy for developing organic constancy?

Stage II: sensory organization

The baby spends most of its waking time organizing sensory input into meaningful, recognizable wholes. In the brain, different sensory areas begin to communicate with each other, when (and only when) properly stimulated they build an internal communication network. The first task a baby faces is to build a coherent sensory system, able to suppress irrelevant information and attending to useful information. The separate sensory faculties (vision, hearing, smell, taste, vestibular information, tactile information, and information from internal organs, muscles and joints) are stimulated by daily care routines, and the mother constantly provides a stabilizing filter, a boundary against the world. She inhibits too violent sensory impressions, and provides external stimulation if the environment is too dull, avoiding sensory deprivation. She gradually teaches the child to endure frustration (hunger, pain, thirst, etc.) by gently postponing the point of satiation and relief.

The functions arising in the child are: ability to sort internal and external information and know which is which (the first boundary is a sensory boundary), to combine different impressions into meaningful wholes, supported by the external routines (e.g. to combine a certain smell, taste, contour, touch, voice and movement into a coherent, recognizable concept of the mother), and to direct attention towards useful stimuli (the breast, the mothers voice, etc.). In short, the child enables itself to have a map of its own internal needs, its boundaries and the important parts of the surroundings (stimuli vital to need fulfillment). The strategies of learning at this stage are recognizing and experimenting with the same stimulation source, movement or figure repeatedly, such as sucking the breast.

The result of this development may be called *sensory constancy*: The faculty of *forming a figure and its background* – the *ability to*

Stage development and diagnosis

In the real world, these 5 stages develop simultaneously – even the newborn has limited social skills such as a readiness for eye contact – but different areas in the brain are activated with increasing age, which is probably why some activities are more promoting to development at certain ages. The model, however, is important in order to organize the focus of therapy and to give 5 different angles for treating the AD child. Versatility in method is the objective.

An example: Jack is destructive and disorganized at the dinner table. We now have 5 different angles and therefore 5 different therapeutic strategies:

Is Jack having organic problems?

Is he unable to control his attention, or unable to perceive that he needs food? Is he having discrete intermittent epileptic seizures (many AD children have this problem)? Does he suffer from a loss of hearing due to frequent inflammation of the middle ear early in life? Does he need glasses? Is he fully awake or is he hyper/hypo-active? Can he direct his attention towards important goals and for how long? Does he have normal reflexes and normal muscle tension?

Is Jack having sensory problems?

Is he so disturbed by noises and movement that he is unable to focus on eating? Is he itching all over the body, because he cannot suppress skin stimuli? Is he shocked by a bitter taste and only wants to eat soft, sweet food? Is he able to feel, when he has had enough food? Does he feel any pain if he falls or cuts himself?

Is Jack having sensory-motor problems?

Does he perform everything in a clumsy, primitive way; spilling the milk, chewing by using the tongue instead of the jaws? Is he able to sit still on a chair anywhere at all? Can he plan holding fork and knife and hit the mouth? Does he still use right and left hand randomly?
Does he push others involuntarily and start fights that way? Does he use his hands as shovels, or can he use his fingers independently? Can he maintain a normal body posture? Does he have body balance problems?

Is Jack having personality problems?

Does he "boil over" when facing normal frustration levels? Can he remember what his role models told him about how to hold a fork, and can he try to do so for some time? Does he eat more precisely and calmly when alone with one adult? Can he decide on how to behave and hold that intention for some time? Can he foresee the knife and fork problems and have a dialogue with himself or with an adult about them? Can he suppress his emotions when things don't go his way and try another strategy? Does he simply imitate trouble behavior when the others do so, or can he have an independent personal intention and meaning? Does he ever express sorrow, grief, shame, guilt, doubt, and fear of separation or fear of strangers? Can he remember what to do in a situation? Is there any connection between words and action, or is he "parrot-talking" without understanding the meaning of his own sentences?

Is Jack having social problems?

Is he unaffected when being in a new environment? Does he understand what is going on in a group? Does he attach to certain adults and other children, or are his contacts many, short, superficial and quickly forgotten? Is he afraid of being alone and abandoned? How many of the social relationships at the table can he cope with, and how does he use his knowledge – is he manipulating towards other children? How does he react when other children are sad, weak or angry? Does he go along with your suggestions or does he lock into primitive opposition (fight/flight/freeze behavior) instead of negotiation? Are his behavior patterns few and stereotype or varied and modified according to the situation? Can he recognize a situation or a room, or does he have to learn the same all over again in new situations and places? Can he wait for his turn?

Naturally, these questions must be answered by comparing Jack's problems with the normal development, and by excluding other diagnoses with similar symptoms.

Only when a child has been described from all five angles can we decide what to do and choose a working model. It is almost useless to treat a socially disobedient child with social behavior modification, if it is unable to hear, or unable to concentrate on what you are saying.

An example: One of the therapeutic units had constant trouble during meals. Everybody analyzed their own behavior and feelings and the children relationships, looking for sources of conflict. Nothing helped. One day the physiotherapist (who works with sensory integration problems) visited the dining room and immediately pointed out that the walls were covered with white tiles. She suggested some carpets in neutral colors on the walls to subdue the echoes. At the next meal, and all later, peace fell over the table to a normal degree. This was a sensory problem, not a deep psychological one. So, working at the right therapeutic level is crucial to successful interventions.

What makes this insight even more necessary is the fact that under pressure, the AD child often copes by regression, i.e. solving problems by functioning at a lower stage of development. Furthermore, these children have the problem of uneven development. They may be normally developed when speech is estimated, 7 years behind when emotional development is estimated, 1 year behind in other areas. Treatment must be differentiated and demands made according to the present task and ability of the child. You may talk calmly about intellectual problems with a 12-year old AD boy, then you touch an emotional subject, and he immediately reacts like a 2-year old,

An example:

Robert came to our institution from a deprived home at the age of 7. He was extremely hyperactive and did not know even the simplest daily functions, such as getting up, how to dress, brush his teeth and so forth. For 6 months, Robert was trained in "getting up": the same person woke him up at the same time every day, his clothes were always lined up on the bed from A to Z, he was followed to the bathroom and gradually learned how to wash and dry himself, look at his face in the mirror in order to learn about his own appearance, and after dressing was followed to the morning table, meeting the other children in his group of ten.

After these 6 months he was slowly learning how to do this by himself. One problem of constancy appeared very suddenly. For two months he had been washing himself alone, but one morning he destroyed everything in the bathroom.

The cause of the problem was that someone had put a brown towel in the bathroom instead of the usual white one. This little background change caused Robert to be unable to recognize the bathroom and to think that he had landed on the moon. He immediately burst into a psychotic episode, and it took some explanation and talking to convince him that the bathroom was the same, even with another kind of towel.

That is how fragile many AD children are in their conception of the "hostile" world around them.

Contact disruption and the AD child

Under stable and relevant conditions, all living things have a tendency to organize their elements in ever more intricate patterns, unfolding the possibilities of their genetic code, their physical conditions and their social environment.

However, different kinds of strain or events can reduce or stop this development. A certain event is not necessarily destructive; this depends on the defense mechanisms and the organism's level of function. To the fetus, thalidomide may cause serious damage; to the adult it is a quite harmless medicine for nausea. Exposed to hunger, cold or isolation, the newborn can only live for hours while the adult may live for weeks or days. Separation for 14 days may cause delayed brain development in the baby, and be a natural thing for the 12-year old.

We do not know for sure what causes an AD personality development. A small portion of all AD children may even be suffering from purely genetic deficits; the underlying mechanisms of these being only on the verge of being mapped. For example, some genes control substances in the brain inhibiting nervous impulses – so, a child may be born "genetically" more or less impulse-ridden. But we can list a number of types of events up to the age of two that are characteristic of the early life conditions of the AD child, but not common for children in general; events, which for the normal child would normally occur much later in life, if at all. Perhaps it is only a question of quantity: the number of contact disrupting events adds up to a point, where emotional development is arrested in early phases.

If the physical or emotional needs of the child are ignored or overruled the child turns its energy away from development and play, into defense, survival or simple fulfillment of needs. Development is, so to speak, a surplus phenomenon, accelerating whenever the child is satisfied and in a state of internal balance. A moderate frustration of needs (as when having to learn to sleep alone) is probably also necessary in order to enhance independence. But AD children usually have been forced to cope with quite intolerable levels of frustration, while their needs scarcely have been fulfilled.

Abnormal contact between mother and child – results from studies

The common trait in mothers of AD children is a reduced sensitivity to the child's needs, a lack of empathy (when does the child need what, and with what speed and intensity), and a lack of ability to maintain a recognizable daily rhythm from which the child can learn (sleep rhythms, feeding rhythms, when to change the diaper, etc.), and a lack of accessibility.

These variations of inadequate contact are common in the early lives of AD children, and are usually a mix of them all. The two basic adaptation mechanisms, described by Piaget (1936), assimilation and accommodation, deteriorate, and instead the child practices avoidance or defense. The child does not develop the ability to adapt itself to changes in the environment (accommodation), and obsessively tries to change its surrounding conditions (assimilation). Usually, it will imitate the environment instead of understanding it, and aggressively destroy the surroundings when feeling threatened. Or, as some depressive types do, give up contact and let others or "whatever happens" decide everything.

Some of the following data are gathered from different studies, especially a longitudinal study by this author of 48 AD children (Rygaard 1998). The study was started in 1988 in a public foster home dedicated to the treatment of AD children, "Himmelbjerggaarden" in

Denmark. The children in question were admitted at the age of 7–14 years by parents, social authorities, and children's psychiatric wards, and they had been diagnosed AD beforehand by professionals.

This group of children has a social bias, since more wealthy parents would likely see private practitioners or cope with the child themselves. All children in the study belonged to lower middle class or poor families.

Lacking other longitudinal studies specifically dealing with the life course of AD children, the reader will hopefully forgive the frequent quotations from this study. It can only give hints to the possible causes. On the other hand, quite a lot of studies have been conducted to investigate the *adult* "AD" person who in the most severe cases is usually diagnosed with the terms "Psychopathic" or "Antisocial Personality Disorder".

There are many different theories about the causes of abnormal social behavior. The major difference between these theories is the size of their scope, i.e. are they looking at micro-cosmic events (what goes on in the cells of a child, making it behave abnormally) or at micro-cosmic events (what goes on in groups or in society that makes a child behave abnormally)? You can say that in some theories the scientist is positioned very close to the subject (genetics), in other theories the child is seen from a distance as part of a larger entity (family, school, etc.). In the growth process of a child it is relevant to see the start of life mainly from a genetic viewpoint, the first years from a neurological viewpoint, and later development from a personality and social perspective. The text is ordered in this manner.

The reader should be aware that these theories have no common denominator, although scientists are trying to find methods to compare data from one discipline with those of another. "Attachment Disorder" can be defined in each theory, for example as a purely neurological problem. However, the major cause is generally agreed to be the consequences of a lack of care in the first interplay between caretaker and child.

Given the imperfect and fragmented scientific evidence, the "Conclusions" should be read as "what seems reasonable to believe".

The genetic background

The embryo has 23 pairs of chromosomes, containing the "script" for the coming individual: sex, body structure and organ structure, eye and hair color, etc. Each pair of chromosomes is built up by numerous genes (specific information), each coded by four bases in different combinations. The genes are ordered in a double helix, forming the chromosome. On this helix, certain genes control series of other genes. After conception, a certain group of cells called "the organizer" takes control of development in the embryo. In this context, it is especially important that the genetic code of the embryonic cell decides the structure of the nervous system and metabolism. A certain hormone balance or a fault in the nervous system can be hereditary.

It is well known that hereditary deficits may cause arrested psychological development, e.g. the Down's syndrome child suffers from a genetic deficit, and seldom develops past the age of 5 in psychological function.

The question of hereditary deficits in AD development has not yet been sufficiently answered, but there are certain hints. Schalling (1968) and others have found a low or unstable production of serotonin in some adult psychopaths. Serotonin is an inhibitor in brain processes, and a lowered serotonin production may cause impulsive and aggressive behavior, one characteristic of the AD personality (Coleman 1971, Higley 1990).

Schulsinger (1972) studied 57 adults diagnosed as psychopaths, who had been admitted to normal foster homes within a year after birth. He then traced their biological parents and found that 58 parents had been admitted to a hospital and had been diagnosed "AD". Then he found a control group of 57 normal adults, who had also lived in foster homes from the age of 1. In this group, only 37 of their biological parents had been diagnosed as psychopaths.

In a study of 3687 seven year old twin pairs, Viding et al. (Viding 2005) distinguished between two groups of children showing antisocial behavior. The specific traits of extreme callous and unemotional behavior proved to be under strong genetic influence, whereas antisocial behavior in general had no genetic connection. Roughly, we can say that the majority of AD children have problems controlling emotion (children with problems due to a lack of proper care and socialization), whereas a minor group of children have problems mobilizing emotion and empathy due to an inborn genetic problem. They display preying behavior without any excitement during acts of violence.

These and other results do not point to a general hereditary component in attachment disorder, but probably genetic problems are a component in some subtypes of antisocial behavior. We do not know which exact genes may be determinants, if any can be pointed out.

Are we talking about one or more factors? Should we look into metabolism, certain abnormal traits in the structure of the nervous system, a tendency in the mother to have an insufficient placenta function, or what? One genetic fact seems to be beyond doubt: that roughly *75% of all psychopaths are male and 25% female*. This is probably because boys have two different (XY) chromosomes, where girls have identical (XX) chromosomes. This means that a genetic fault in one chromosome in boys will have no "back-up" from the other. Several studies point to the fact that boys are more vulnerable to many child diseases, and in some respects have prolonged developmental periods, compared to girls. Therefore, the vulnerable and dependent periods of early life are probably longer in boys (Zlotnik 1984, and others).

Also, boys may have a stronger disposition for aggressive and impulsive behavior than girls.

We may conclude that genetic disposition may, in some cases, play an enforcing role in AD development. This has yet to be revealed in greater detail. The major cause in general seems to be the lack of mutual contact in the first years of life.

The course of pregnancy

Out of the 44 mothers in the author's study, 24 had a record of continuous mixed alcohol and drug abuse, and this is one reason to raise the question of mother/fetus contact. Especially alcohol abuse can destroy the finer sensory processing areas in the brain (Fetal Alcohol Effects). This may prevent the baby from perceiving contact and stimulation, since the outcome of F.A.E. is hypersensitivity to stimulation. F.A.E.-babies cry at normal levels of sensory impressions. They often lose weight, since they are not able to suck normally, and often have serious digestion problems. They cry if someone talks loudly or shuts a door, they overreact to touch. Later in life, they often become hyperactive and have learning problems.

Stress during pregnancy has not been sufficiently investigated, yet Mirdal (1976) can identify items such as sensory hypersensitivity, exaggerated alarm responses and eating difficulties in newborn babies, whose mothers were excessively stressed during pregnancy.

Birch (Lou 1976) has studied the consequences of malnutrition. In animals, a smaller cranium, a reduced number of nervous cells, a tendency towards hypersensitivity and an excessive activity level has been found.

In practice, many disrupting circumstances could be seen in the life of the 44 mothers.

Especially the AD and psychotic mothers were unable to sleep and rest regularly, or to eat according to the needs of pregnancy. They often exposed themselves to violence and to violent events, unable to take care of themselves.

> I interviewed one mother about her pregnancy, and this illustrates very well the AD mother's attitude towards care and self-care. I asked her if she had experienced any stress during pregnancy, and she said that this was not the case. I then asked her whether she had hurt herself, and she replied, "Well, I fell off a running motorbike because I was drunk – that was in my fifth month ... and later our neighbor had repaired the electric stove, and I almost got electrocuted when I turned it on ... I passed out for 20 minutes ... that was a week before I delivered him – is that what you mean by 'stress'?"

One conclusion could be that mothers of AD children more often than other mothers expose themselves and the fetus to extreme life conditions, have a higher tendency to be alcohol abusers, and do not eat properly during pregnancy. This may produce a child with severe contact problems and lowered receptivity to stimulation combined with a tendency towards hyperactivity, and also a lower ability to learn from experience.

The course of birth

One way of measuring the quality of pregnancy is the criterion of birth weight.

The average birth weight in Denmark for children born in the same period as the sample in the study was 3344 gr, and for the sample group it was 3028 gr, an average difference of 316 gr. None of the 47 children in sample weighed more than 4000 gr, compared to 11% in the average population. 17% weighed less than 2.500 gr, compared to only 6% in the average population. This difference was even larger when compared to a control group of 23 normal children. Figure 1 illustrates birth weight in the sample compared with control group and with average birth weight in all Danish children born in the same period as the sample.

Kruuse (1984) followed 340 children with low birth weight (less than 2.500 gr.), compared to a control group of 240 children with normal birth weight. The children were born 1959–1961 and were examined with reference to the course of their school education 1977–78. The study showed that the children with low birth weight

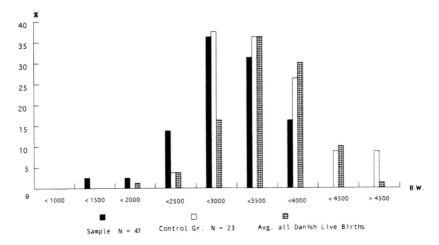

Fig. 1. Birth weight in sample, control group and Danish average

left school earlier and that fewer graduated than the control group. 8 times as often they had had to attend special learning disability classes. As in other studies, boys proved most vulnerable: double as many low weight boys as girls left school without graduating.

The course of the birth process is crucial in life. The child must give up many forms of external support, and must activate internal functional systems. Out of the 48 children, many had experienced serious birth complications, compared to the average for all Danish births (Table 2).

From the records it was obvious that many of the children had secondary problems. 3 had continuous fever convulsions after birth (sometimes a fore-runner of epileptic seizures). 1 was asphyxiated, 2

Table 2. Frequency of birth complications and artificial birth aid

	Sample (%)	Normal (%)
Preeclampsia	8.5	1.3
Preterm birth (> 3 weeks)	11.0	4.0
Forceps	2.1	0.7
Episiotomia	12.5	?
Membrane rupt.	10.5	?
Membrane punct.	6.2	?
Pudendus	14.5	?

had respiratory problems. 5 caught meningitis within a year after birth. 2 had to be placed in an incubator for several weeks.

Zachau (1975) followed a group of children with birth complications and found several secondary complications such as a high infection frequency that further delayed the development of the child.

Hansen (1977) examined a group of 110 children, admitted to a children's psychiatric ward. He found that children who had both a history of organic dysfunction caused by birth/pregnancy problems as well as a very weak social and emotional upbringing would be diagnosed as having AD. This caused him to denote this condition "organic psycho-syndrome". Children who had only one of these characteristics were liable to have other diagnoses.

We may conclude that mother/child contact in AD children is often disturbed already during pregnancy and birth, in many causing organic dysfunction. That the child will often suffer from early disease and functional disturbances during the first years. The effects of child problems will be enforced by the lowered contact and care ability in the mother.

> One of the mothers told us about a complicated birth and her own reactions, "I told them at the hospital that he was small, red and ugly (he was prematurely born), and that they could keep him until he looked like a normal kid. So I went home for two weeks. When I came to get him, he was still too small and cried all the time – I don't think he liked me, and I didn't like him much either. So I tried to feed him because he wouldn't eat. I put more powder in his milk bottle than they told me to at the hospital – so he got diarrhea, and I had to take him back to them".

CHAPTER 4

CONTACT DISRUPTION AND NERVOUS SYSTEM DEVELOPMENT

Central nervous system (CNS) development

In adult psychopaths, several studies indicate abnormal and unstable CNS (Central Nervous System) brain function (Hare 1985, Christiansen 1972), such as absent or delayed arousal (the ability to react quickly to stimulation by mobilizing energy, a state of wakefulness and attention to stimuli), a high frequency of epilepsy, and the easily observable lack of impulse inhibition.

If you look at the abovementioned, some childhood foundations of this instability/immaturity may be implied. But there is more evidence that deprivation and other abnormal early contact may cause the brain to remain functionally unstable and undeveloped. What seems to be most destructive to the first year of CNS-development is when *touch* (tactile stimulation) and *being moved* (vestibular stimulation, body balance) is excluded from the baby's communication experiences.

Reide (1979) found in laboratory experiments with chimpanzees that maternal deprivation of touch for periods of 14 days (short term separation) during the first year caused chronically disturbed rhythms in brain and body functions. This was found even when only touching contact with the mother was prevented. The chimpanzee and her baby could still see, smell and hear each other, but a window was between them. Abnormal EEG patterns, unstable patterns of breathing, sleeping, eating, heart rhythm were found and this instability continued even when the "child" was put back with the mother, and apparently felt comforted again. Also, lowered immune function and a following higher frequency of early disease were found (Laudenslager 1982). These physical instabilities were not found when only bars separated mother and baby, allowing them to touch and to cling to each other.

Chimpanzees who as babies had been separated with respect to touch during the first year for periods of 14 days (short term separation) developed as adults an insecure, care-seeking and frightened behavior (translated into human terms: a neurotic fear of separation). They would constantly cling to each other, and not engage in normal activities such as grooming, play, searching for food and variation. Babies that were continually separated during the first year (long term separation) developed aggressive fight/flight behavior, could not recognize other monkeys, and could not subordinate to the social rules of the chimpanzee society, and were therefore avoided by others. They were a-social.

In another study, a loss of development in the limbic system (containing the areas of emotional function) was found. Normally, nervous cells communicate by connecting dendrites, when the brain is stimulated in normal interaction with the mother. But both in the short-and long-term separated chimpanzees, dendrite development was arrested or greatly delayed in the limbic system (Heath 1975, Bryan 1989). This probably means that the internal communication network formed by connecting dendrites does not develop properly when the baby is separated from the mother. The scientists are convinced that this also applies in humans, since the similarities between man and chimpanzees, concerning the first development of the CNS, are many especially regarding the function of the limbic system. The consequences of reduced dendrite growth following early separation probably are that the neurological "internal network" between different functional areas of the brain becomes imprecise and unstable. Recent studies seem to indicate a critical period for brain networks to form in the prefrontal cortex from 10–18 months, linking emotional responses with higher areas of the brain, so to speak forming the possibility of combining thinking, planning and language with feeling. The success of this linking apparently depends on proper parental communication and care.

In the brain the Reticular Activation System (R.A.S.) is crucial to normal brain development and to adequate response to the environment. The R.A.S. is so to speak the area that activates the rest of the brain. You may call it the "start-and-stop button" for brain activation. Its function is called arousal; the mobilization of brain activity, including attention-, pulse-, breath-, gland-, hormone-activity. This R.A.S. provides a state of proper awareness, concentration and onward. All higher and more complex intellectual functions, including inhibition of the two lower brain units, and the ability to be empathic, are programmed here through contact with mother and other important persons in the group, mainly to the age of 14. Refined and complex movement is located here: language and motor control of fingers, lips and tongue. The frontal lobes perform all more complex control of the whole brain, including modulation and suppression of impulses from other areas in the brain.

If the frontal lobes are compromised, the person will in many ways show psychopathic and impulse-ridden behavior, having lost the "center of final control".

There are 4 major causes for compromised frontal lobe function:

1. Physical trauma – as seen in car accidents and working accidents.
2. Exposition to alcohol or other fat-dissolving liquids – as seen in Fetal Alcohol Syndrome, or other organic solvents.
3. Lowered activity level in the brain – as seen in under-stimulated babies.
4. Infections affecting brain tissue.

This part of the brain develops later (1–14 years) than the limbic part, and this may explain why intelligence is relatively unaffected in many psychopaths. Contact disruption has primarily affected the "emotional programming" areas, and not so much the intellectual development, depending on stimulation later in life.

The prefrontal Cortex seems to play a major part in controlling the emotional processes of the limbic brain, and the successful development of emotional control depends heavily on proper caregiver/baby communication. According to Schore (Schore 2002), the mother exercises emotional control by helping the baby become excited and calm down in an empathic way.

If this communication does not take place regularly from 10–18 months, the prefrontal Cortex fails in learning to control the Amygdala, the "alarm state" center of the limbic brain. The child will then later be unable to soothe itself or control the intensity of emotion in general (a little fear will often end in a state of overexcited panic).

A number of types of stress (as yet, we don't know which are the most disruptive) cause a lack of neurological programming and maturation of brain functional systems in the AD child. The most fatal lack of development is in the limbic system, where basic emotional programming and learning should have taken place. The limbic system is probably most receptive to programming from birth to the age of 2, which is the age where AD children usually have suffered the most from abnormal contact. The lack of inhibition from the limbic and neo-cortical areas makes the child more apt to exert predatory and uninhibited behavior, elicited from the reptile brain system.

We may conclude that the early environmental conditions for CNS-development and functional neurological organization have usually been very poor for the AD child. We may hypothesize that the neurological consequences in severe cases may be: arrested development of functional brain systems, such as unstable basic body rhythms, lowered immune function and frequent early diseases. A possible dominance of reptile system aggressive and defensive behavior, "social blindness" due to a lack of limbic system programming, and a lack of ability to analyze and react to sensory stimulation (arousal deficits).

Checklist for deprivation symptoms in babies

This list is a supplement for your own common-sense observations. A single symptom may be no cause for alarm. You should always be aware that these symptoms might have other causes as well, such as a temporary crisis or disease.

Insufficient attachment behavior and lack of response

The baby doesn't respond when you attempt to have eye contact. The eyes do not focus on your face or change according to your facial expression. The baby seems to avoid eye contact and physical contact intentionally, or contact is disrupted in the middle of initiation. Normally, a baby will respond by imitating your facial expression (with a 5–30 seconds delay).

Here, you only meet avoidance or a lack of response. The toddler may expose paradoxical attachment behavior when starting a contacting sequence (such as moving towards an adult to seek comfort), but the child interrupts this behavior half-way, and may bang the head against the wall, turn around and run away, have a temper tantrum, etc. When sitting on the lap, the toddler may prefer to be turning its back on you. The point is that you are perceived by the child as both a caregiver – and at the same time as a potential danger.

This psychological conflict is a blind alley to the child and therefore results in paradoxical contact patterns (fight/flight), where the need for care and the fear of separation, violence or abuse are in conflict.

Depression: lowered muscle tonus

"Depression" in the clinical sense of the word is a physiological term meaning "a low processing speed and activity level", whereas in psychology "depression" refers to a mood or state of feeling. In the child, a lack of stimulation (particularly physical contact and body movement, such as being rocked in the cradle) will cause depression, one symptom being lowered muscle tension. The postural reflexes (unfolding the body towards upright, standing position) are not sufficiently elicited, and the child sinks back into the fetus position.

The child can't lift the head when lying on the stomach or standing on all four, can't sit upright at the appropriate developmental thresholds (hypotonic).

Un-stabilized basic body rhythms

When the baby has not been rocked and touched sufficiently, the general activity level in the brain will be lowered resulting in unstable basic body rhythms that normally would appear only in the newborn. Rhythms, such as heartbeat, breath, body temperature regulation, attention, deep relaxation and sleep versus focused alert attention, digestion (including appetite, bladder and bowl control) will not stabilize over time if the baby is under stimulated. Symptoms are sometimes death (due to arrested cardiac activity and lack of appetite and failure of digestion processes), in milder cases problems of hyper-or hypo-activity, eating disorders and a general lack of ability to cope with external change and achieve emotional stability. Also, touch and vestibular stimulation facilitate growth hormone production, and psychosocial dwarfism may be another symptom (small head circumference, lowered weight and height development).

Lowered or permanently stressed immune function

The lack of early physical stimulation and separation experiences can lead to an improper immune function; the symptom being that the baby and later toddler is overly receptive to disease of any kind (lowered T-cell production and -differentiation). The child's case record will often be filled with a list of diseases, and colic, diarrhea and catching colds will appear frequently.

In milder cases, where stress is induced by separation after learning to recognize the mother, frequent traumatic separation experiences can induce a generally hyperactive immune function, the symptoms being a tendency towards asthma, allergies, rash and juvenile arthritis.

In several studies, adults exposed to traumatic separations in childhood have an earlier onset of heart diseases, diabetes and other stress-related diseases than do non-traumatized adults.

CHAPTER 5

ABNORMAL SENSORY-MOTOR DEVELOPMENT IN THE TODDLER

Sensation, attention, emotion, gestalt formation: the basics of learning

Learning something (and remembering it) has at least 4 basic premises:

The baby is able to focus attention towards important stimuli, is able to process and sort the stimuli, and is able to experience an internal emotional reaction to sensation (like or dislike, become excited or calm, love, experience longing or rejection, etc.).

The child is able to *respond* to stimulation (a motor activity), and a feedback loop is created between mother and child.

These basic abilities will be enhanced, praised and rewarded by the normal mother – a hundred times a day – from the moment of birth and a few years on, until they have been internalized by the toddler.

The functions developed in the baby by maternal care are the ability to form meaningful wholes, focus and concentrate, give undivided lasting attention, receiving comfort enough to have curiosity and appropriate fear, recognize, display experimenting and explorative behavior, exchange information and emotion, and synchronize emotional expressions and gestures. These functions are in short: the basics of learning. We don't readily realize that they are basically built and stabilized during the first year of life, in cooperation with loving adults.

The abovementioned neurological characteristics, combined with a lack of attention from the mother during the first years, may be the cause of the short attention span, constant boredom and news-seeking behavior in AD children. Because of poor processing abilities, the child is isolated from receiving, processing and "digesting" sensory information and therefore seeks what looks like over stimulation in order to feel stimulated at all. The child is unable to form a precise "gestalt"; a stable internal fantasy about what can fulfill a particular need. It will contact anything or anyone without being able to derive lasting pleasure or satisfaction from the contact. It has no other choice than to contact again and again. AD children try to have contact all the time, but in vain, or they give up all contact.

Often, deprived children will appear depressive until the age of 2 or 3, after which most become hyperactive, with a compulsive drive for frequent, restless contact.

In the normal child, you will observe longer periods of attention. A mother or father will try incessantly to prolong and reward periods of attention by waving, smiling, varying voice pitch while keeping an intense focus and exaggerating any emotional reaction from the child. The baby will seek contact with new objects or people roughly every 20 seconds, the one year old will remain longer in contact with an object, attend, study and manipulate it for minutes. The 5 year old can play with an object for about 20 minutes. The AD child will stay briefly in superficial contact with an object or person, and will quickly become bored. This prevents learning in a deeper sense.

The absence of internal emotional reactions and arousal in contact will prevent the process of different sensations forming an experience (helping you in the next similar event). This affects the learning process.

If the child doesn't experience pain or pleasure, joy or sorrow, fear or comfort, all impressions become flat and one-dimensional. It is difficult to remember something if you don't feel an emotional response. The limbic (emotional response) memory is out of order. Children remember first by feeling, and only later as an intellectual experience. This may explain why the AD child does not learn from experience and therefore repeats stereotypical behavior patterns which is unaffected by punishment or reward. Reward and punishment will only work with the normal child who is able to recognize and compare present and past experiences.

Normally, when the organism is off balance by a state of need (hunger, thirst, boredom, loneliness, longing for someone), energy is mobilized as an impulse to fulfill the need. The newborn needs help to direct attention towards the object, get in contact and fulfill the need, withdraw and rest until the next imbalance arises. The more mature the child becomes, the more precision in attention, goal direction, contact discrimination, withdrawal after satisfaction and rest. The contact pattern will become more and more elaborate and contain more and more experience. At the same time, the coherent external feedback will probably cause internal brain circuits to form. Psychologically, the child will learn to form an internal idea, a figure of what can satisfy the need, a gestalt. The quality of precise gestalt formation later in life will of course be based on the quality of early experiences with the most important gestalt, the mother.

Movement and motor development

In order to unfold the inborn movement programs – starting with the reflexes – development is accelerated by physical contact with the mother. One program is the postural reflex. When a baby is placed in an upright position and the feet touch the floor, the postural reflex will make it stretch the body. Or the fall reflex: if the baby falls backwards, it will stretch out the arms and lift the head, etc. The reflexes are simple motor programs, some inherited from other species preceding mankind. Reflexes are developed into planning of motor patterns, and later some will be suppressed if the child is stimulated, e.g. a normal baby will turn the head towards a sound, later it will be able to suppress this reflex if it concentrates on something else. The poor environment of these children usually produces a lowered muscle tone and a delay in the development from reflex to intentional movement and motor planning. The fundamental prerequisite for motor development is sensory stimulation.

What you generally see in young AD children is a tendency towards primitive, compulsive stimulation-reaction patterns. The child can't ignore stimulation and is distracted by any strong source of stimulation in the environment, a here and now reaction. What you also see is the absence of normal automatic habits, such as dressing, brushing teeth, eating, and other daily self-care habits. Simply because the parent has not had regular habits, including those of child rearing, the child will not know the simplest facts about its own body and body function.

An example, a girl with severe arrest in motor development:

Jeanie was five when she came to the institution. She had grown up in very poor surroundings, often locked up alone for hours, sometimes days. She walked like "The Hunchback of Notre Dame", since she could not straighten her back. Her mouth was constantly open, and she could not control her tongue. She walked like a two year old, legs apart, alternately moving one side of the body. Her drawings were scratches with a pencil and she could only hold the pencil between her thumb and the rest of her fingers. She could not keep her head still or follow an object with her eyes. Jeanie knew only a few words and used them in a very generalizing way. She was curious and would often stand behind a door, peeking and listening. After a while (or if you looked at her) she would disappear and be back again a minute later. She never played with toys or showed any interest in other children. She would get up often during the night and head for the refrigerator. She disliked sitting on a lap and preferred to keep some distance. Swimming and massage were the first two treatments. She also did a lot of activities while lying on the stomach (this elicits postural reflexes). Jeanie violently opposed stimulation, whining or tantrumming. She learned quickly, and after a year she knew about a hundred words. She also enjoyed swimming and was able to do a "doggie paddle" stroke by herself. She could now raise her head and see what or who was in front of her.

From birth, Jeanie was unwanted by her mother who was somewhat retarded. The mother tended to treat Jeanie like a puppy, sometimes caressing her violently, sometimes forgetting her due to her own needs. The parents often had violent arguments and tried to choke each other. Jeanie did not have any toys, and the parents would punish her physically, when something went wrong. If she cried she was locked in a closet for a day. This happened frequently from birth on.

As described earlier, AD children often suffer from neurological deficits during pregnancy and birth. A particular group are more often than normal children exposed to parental violence. Vesterdal (1978) and Green (1982) mention premature children, children with a difficult birth, children separated from the mother at the age of 0–6 months, children with minor brain dysfunctions and children deliberately provoking adults. Their explorative behavior and efforts to learn movement will often elicit very negative feedback loops such as random severe punishment which in turn, will arrest motor development and destroy natural exploration and curiosity.

Phases in motor development

The important phases in motor development are excellently described by Gallahue (1997).

The Reflex Movement Phase
(0–4 months, coding sensory information)

A reflex is an involuntary reaction to stimulation, an inborn unconscious motor scheme. To grasp when you are falling, to suck when sensing the breast, to seek balance when you are pushed or moved quickly up or down, etc. The presence of a reflex is part of the

playing, dressing, eating, etc. They tend to perceive their surroundings as dangerous and not as interesting objects. They will often confine exercise to one or two successful activities and avoid other more general play activities. In play they will often try to pull objects or people apart and then loose interest. They will be handicapped in social activities also because of their lack of motor programming.

An example:

James grew up in a criminal, violent family. At the age of three he witnessed his father stab his mother with a kitchen knife. After numerous institutional placements we received him at the age of 12. He was a very intelligent and shrewd boy. His motor development was the equivalent of a six year old. He would hide this behind an aggressive and violent behavior, often bragging about his abilities. His voice was monotonous and mumbling. He could not tell the difference between "k" and "t". When provoked, he would grab any long object and start beating at someone or something, crying "Idiot, you idiot!" When calm, he could charm strangers by imitating their opinions and manners. He would usually have a sadistic intention to hurt a person and experienced joy by hurting others. He would always criticize any activity, behavior, dress or emotion of others. All his actions depended on what was happening at the present moment. If others were calm, he would be calm, if there was excitement or movement, he would panic, become confused and aggressive. Loud talking was enough to excite him. He was obsessive in his need to control others and his initial friendliness was a means to this end.

Checklist for preschool AD symptoms

The basis for developing a mature, discriminating contact pattern is the ability to receive sensory information. AD children very often display sensory deficits, such as:

External sensation

Seeing

- Does not focus eyes on an object or person for very long. Focuses on any moving object, not the relevant object.
- Can't recognize people and facial mood expressions.
- Does not like muted, diffuse or abstract drawings. Prefers strong colors and sharp, simple figures.

Hearing

- Sometimes hears poorly due to early inflammation of the middle ear. Does not respond to verbal instructions, unless you speak loudly. Does not process a verbal direction in the presence of other children or background noise. Attention is drawn to the loudest sound, not the most relevant.

- Does not remember what you say. You have to ask the child to repeat your words.

Boundary sensation

Skin contact

- Does not distinguish between hot and cold.
- Overreacts, avoids, or is indifferent to touch.
- Does not experience pain when falling, e.g. accidentally hitting or burning itself.
- Avoids physical contact with you, or tries to "stick to you" like glue.
- Is often over-stimulated by a shower when bathing, or clothes that have a rough texture.
- Does not dress according to temperature.
- Does not giggle or respond to tickling and touch.

Taste

- Prefers soft food.
- Does not discriminate between different tastes or enjoy/explore taste.
- Eats anything quickly without tasting.
- Dislikes food randomly.

Smell

- Does not differentiate between bad and pleasant scents.
- Sometimes obsessed with strong scents.

Internal sensation

Muscle sensations, kinesthetic sensation

- Is often unable to experience fatigue or over-tense muscles.
- Does not react to internal pain or tired muscles.
- E.g, will fall down the stairs without any following cry or expression of pain.
- Poor appetite regulation (eats beyond satiation or has no appetite at all).

Internal balance, vestibular sensation

- Does not respond or overreacts to vestibular stimulation.
- E.g. can not maintain a standing position with closed eyes.
- Has difficulty climbing hills or descending stairs.
- Can swing for long periods without nausea or feeling dizzy or, falls off after a few seconds.

These traits (or mixtures of such traits) will be most prominent in children who have been deprived and abandoned. They are not often seen in those children exposed to excessive stimulation, such as chaotic and violent homes.

However, almost all AD children will show poor basic sensory discrimination abilities.

They are very alert to what is going on around them and how others feel. This poor "sensory body map" is probably the forerunner of the poor awareness of the self in personality development. A simple thing like knowing that "I" can be the cause of something happening is a problem of the AD child.

CHAPTER 6

ARRESTED EMOTIONAL PERSONALITY DEVELOPMENT

Personality development: the object relationship is the key to the world. Achieving object constancy

The following paragraphs are further developments of the inspiring papers by S. Blatt (Blatt 1988) who has studied childhood causes of personality disorders. His interest is the notion that cognitive development depends on emotional roots, created in the first relationship to an object, the mother/caretaker. We learn in a deeper sense *by heart*, i.e. the first emotional structures form the base of psychological functioning in general.

Normal sensory-motor development in a secure relationship will produce the unfolding of general psychological functions. Personality function is intimately connected with early concrete experiences of contact. The AD child is unable to form effective mutual relationships – because it can't clearly perceive (a sensory ability) and can't adequately respond (a complex motor activity).

From birth and on, the mother-child relationship is a protected area where the two constantly give each other feedback and attune with each other. In this protected world, stable concepts of the mother are formed. This is initially an emotional process which then develops into cognitive skills.

We receive millions of stimuli each second. How do we discern the important from the unimportant ones? Of course, we learn this by having an emotional center right in front of our eyes for the first year of life. This adds emotional "gravity" to some information and less to some. This is how we basically learn "how to learn". In the first years of constant communication with the caretakers, we constantly receive help to:

–   conceptualize
–   focus
–   recognize
–   learn from experience
–   concentrate
–   communicate
–   respond
–   engage emotionally
–   endure frustration
–   build an emotional "working model of what a person is"

These are basic skills for building stable concepts and a stable personality. AD children can be very intelligent or not, but these poorly developed skills will always be their Achilles heel. If you can only concentrate for a minute, don't know where to focus and how to maintain focus. If you are unable to recognize a situation, if you can't respond adequately, if you are only motivated for a short while, if you give up as soon as something is difficult, how can you learn in a deeper and more profound sense?

If you look at the normal child, having received proper early feedback, the baby can look at the mother for a few seconds, but her tireless response will create still longer periods of concentration. At age one the child can concentrate looking at her for perhaps a few minutes. At age three it can play with the same toy for perhaps fifteen minutes, in school it can concentrate on a book or play with a friend for half an hour, as a teenager it can keep a partner for several months.

The cornerstone of a simple function such as concentration has been stabilized in the first relationship with the caretaker and the function is then a general key to an ordered and sensible contact with the environment in general.

The first stages in achieving object constancy

Object constancy means that emotions endure for longer periods. Stable emotions allow the baby to have stable intentions and ideas about what is important (internal concepts and goals). Stable ideas and concepts will produce stable, intentional behavior. Thanks to this development, the toddler can ignore random events in the present environment and stick to intention.

Basic object constancy develops particularly during the first three years of life. It passes through a number of developmental stages; the first two are most relevant for understanding severe AD.

Stages I and II: basic attachment and basic anxiety management

1. Evocative constancy (0–6 months).
Basic attachment

Emotions are still evoked more by the presence of the mother. She becomes the emotional "figure", everything else becomes "background". Since perception is not very precise, the "mother" is not necessarily a certain person, but someone who communicates in the same caretaking way. The object relationship is being formed as a specific set of emotional reactions when the caretaker is near.

2. Border constancy (6–12 months).
Anxiety management

Now perception is more developed, the baby can separate "known" and "unknown" people, and remember the mother even though she leaves the room for a short while. Consequently, fear of strangers and fear of separation enter life. Emotions are insecure when new people are introduced or when familiar people leave.

Learning to perceive and focus on the mother helps the child organize tools for perceiving all future objects and people in the environment. The child will at first learn to separate the maternal gestalt from the background. A little later, he/she will be able to perceive and concentrate on environmental objects all together (like a rattle), since she has now obtained borders – and figure/background constancy. The child examines the different aspects of the mother (eyes, mouth, hair, smell, movements, etc.) and learns to recognize them. She is now able to know whether she is held by her mother or by someone unknown. Consequently she reacts with fear and tears to separation and strange people. A little later in development she will prefer well-known objects to unknown and have a need for repetition and recognizable surroundings. She now has constancy of recognition. In this phase the threat to the baby is the horrible fear when discovering for the first time that mother can "disappear", and the baby can feel totally abandoned. This is something experienced by any toddler when being put to bed, but she will learn to control the fear if the parents can be empathic and make daily separations a gradual process, and not a traumatizing experience.

Again, perceiving the world depends on learning to perceive the mother in an organized way.

The creation of constancy is primarily an emotional process motivated by the mother (the object), and then unfolds as a cognitive ability, which is used to perceive *all* objects in the world.

Children who have not had qualified contact at these two initial stages will be poorly able to form meaningful emotional and conceptual working models of "the other" and personal relationships and they will frequently be diagnosed AD later in life.

An example: poor basic attachment

When deprived in the first stage, the later child/adult person will become schizoid and psychotically disorganized when frustrated, especially when close emotional contact is offered or and borders and limits are not clear.

The child will have little sense of borders between itself and the surroundings, be unable to organize impressions, and will often become symbiotic with the environment.

He/she will not attach to you at all and only be aware of your existence when you are present, and will often only respond to direct touch. The child will have practically no self-awareness. The child will display many emotional reactions, but only from moment to moment.

> We received Ann at age 11 from a foster family. The emotional contact had been stressed and the parents tried to evoke love, guilt and attachment. They tried to "get as close to her as possible". The fragile girl had reacted with psychotic episodes; setting the house on fire, screaming for hours, performing bizarre rituals, making strange noises, etc. We created a kind and invariable regime, telling her exactly what she should do and when, we preferred rules to emotional motivation. After a week she had improved and become a functioning AD girl. Now Ann was able to attend our on-site school, and only had short, non-involving, practical relationships. Towards strangers she was very charming and contacted anyone indiscriminatingly. Ann had been abandoned by her mother immediately after birth. Her history was unknown until she was delivered to an orphanage at age two and placed with foster parents.

Another example:

> James is twelve years old. His complexion is pale; his eyes are cold and observing.
> He does not express emotion except when unpredictably enraged. In tests he is highly intelligent, yet when he experiences contact his behavior seems appropriate for a baby. This is a passage he wrote, describing a situation on the playground, "We were on the playground and then Brian took Thomas' skateboard and ran off and then I took it and ran away and then Thomas hit

me with a shoe and then I took Brian's books and then Thomas took a shoe and went after Brian and then I told Thomas I would take it from him and, but then he said he would throw it on me and then Brian told me to come over and then I did that and then I took a stone and hit Thomas and then the teacher came over".

Clearly, this boy only experiences the moment-to-moment, and is unable to remember or anticipate other situations. The episode resulted in a skull fracture when he "took a stone and hit Thomas". James' mother, and later his stepmother were both strangled by his father before he was 2 years old.

An example: paradoxical attachment and poor anxiety management

If deprived mostly in the second phase, attachment will form during multiple states of panic anxiety (if the parents are violent, unpredictable, sexual abusers, neglecting). On one hand the child will be totally dependent for care; on the other hand the parent will represent a threat by being too violent or otherwise disrespectful of boundaries and limits. Any contact will therefore become very ambivalent. The sense of borders (you/me) will be compromised. Consequently, the child will often become paranoid (believe that its own hostility is coming from the outside). The only safe relationship will be to hate the object; this assures contact and distance at the same time.

The child will project unbearable hostile and depressed feelings onto others and experience these feelings as being directed towards itself, "I know you hate me – you're only 'kind' because you are too weak, and such a coward that you can't even scold me!" When offered contact he will alternate between searching for contact in an obsessive way, only to reject or destroy the contacting person in a split second. He will hate anyone who attempts intimacy. Intimate contact elicits withdrawal/rejection. He will persistently adhere to details or arguments that are not part of a meaningful whole. He will ritualize stereotypical meaningless behavior. The child will enjoy "trapping" or deceiving you or, entangle you in endless discussions about your reasonable demands. He will chronically perceive you as hostile. The child will not be able to remember you or your directions for any length of time. The child will alternate between defining itself in extremely negative or omnipotent terms ("balloon ego").

The primary defense mechanism of this stage is "splitting". Any experience or emotion will be intense and will mobilize counter-emotions which will be difficult to endure. The child is vulnerable to complexity and border phenomena (is this "me" or "the other"?), and reacts by reducing the difficult graduations by dividing everything into antagonistic pairs, such as good/bad, strong/weak, me/others, mine/yours.

Jealousy can be a predominant emotion, caused by the perceived danger of a possible loss if the "mother's" attention disappears. The children trapped in this phase often perceive you as alternatively totally nice or totally evil depending on the situation. They can't unite these two perceptions into one, a realistic idea about you as a person having both qualities at the same time. They often develop sadistic and hyper controlling contact patterns and have difficulty recognizing strong emotions as their own. One variant of this pattern is the "Münchhausen by Proxy" syndrome, where mothers project their chaos and pain onto the baby, repeatedly hurting it (in accordance with their own unconscious experience of pain), and insisting that something is wrong with the baby, taking him to numerous hospitals. If the mother is suicidal, she may kill the baby. She will experience herself as being free of pain and symptoms by projecting them onto the child (projective identification).

> Charles (ten years old) arrived (after attending numerous schools and institutions) at our institution during a lunch break. He stands seething with anger and suddenly yells at me: "You can't force me to eat, fuck you!" I answer, "Charles, nobody will force you to eat … if you want to eat, there is food on the table. After one o'clock, the food will be taken away", and he replies, "You idiot, you can't force me not to eat either!"
>
> One minute he is extremely compulsive and everything must be in its proper place. The next minute he will destroy his room, his belongings, or start a fight. In class, he is met by his new teacher, Iris. At their first meeting, she kindly says to him: "Hello, Charles – could we write a list about why you will hate me today?" They do this and create a 15 item list. Next, Iris asks him to list how he will sabotage the school lessons; this adds up to 12 strategies. Next, Iris says, "Well, let's start then, shall we?" For over a year, Charles faithfully reproduces the two original lists. Iris is always kind, she never gives in, she never scolds him and she takes any decision needed. After the first year, Charles has accepted the inevitable; Iris is much stronger than Charles (proved through many tests on his behalf) and virtually impossible to provoke. He is now able to work during class and rises quickly to a cognitive level appropriate for his age. He is enrolled in a normal public school while continuing to stay with us.

Another example:

> Frederick is nine years old. His mother suffered from a perinatal psychosis and experienced intense feelings of guilt from this. Consequently she still tries to treat him as a baby in a symbiotic style. When he arrives at our

between the loyalty towards his mother, and her paranoid, deluded view of others, and the care he was offered at the institution. He was permanently in opposition towards staff members and other children, claiming that he had been misplaced. When meeting with his mother they would usually sit at a distance from each other. Allen would try to suppress his need for care and she would indirectly warn him not to come closer or to express affection. In monologues about how to behave she would talk about "the duties of mothers and the duties of children".

Conclusions to background: the general AD risk checklist

The following items, based on studies and experience, are common traits in the AD child's developmental background. It is important to emphasize that a child may be exposed to these forms of contact disruption and still come become a child who is able to attach to others. This uncertainty is due to the fact that no single factor eliciting emotional development arrest can be determined. It is also due to the lack of scientific studies in this field. However, when more background traits can be recognized, the more reason to consider a preventive effort or have a professional conduct a psychiatric evaluation or a psychological assessment which includes the Rorschach test.

The list is helpful when taking a client's early history as a part of your diagnosis. It can be used as a basis for structuring your interviews with parents and with others who have knowledge of the child. In adoption processes this list can be useful.

Family items

1. The mother has been exposed to early deprivation, violence and/or sexual abuse as a child.
2. The mother changes partner frequently. Her relationships are short and superficial. She has a tendency towards isolation from the environment or is in perpetual conflict.
3. There is a family tendency towards psychopathy or psychosis and the mother has been psychotic in the early life of the child.
4. A normal mother who, during the child's first two years was exposed to a crisis, impeding the maternal care. This is less frequently the case.

    There is evidence of some organic deficits preventing the child from sensing and ordering the feedback given in maternal care.

5. The family moves often. The family role pattern is disorganized with no limits to child behavior or with sudden, inconsistent restrictions.

   Frequent sexual abuse between family members and others is seen, due to diffuse sexual orientation ability in parents (polymorphous perversion, arrested oral/anal phase development). Sometimes rigid and void roles are emphasized in order to control the underlying chaotic state.

6. The mother is unable to maintain stable practical and emotional contact with the child.

   The child is often cared for by many different people. Repetitive separations are common.

   Family life lacks a daily rhythm. The mother projects adult motives and emotions onto the child (e.g. "He doesn't like me" about a baby). The mother lacks empathy and blames only others for the child's abnormal development. The mother displays no self-criticism, doubts, and second thoughts, feelings of guilt or remorse.

Violent or sadistic behavior towards the child is sometimes practiced by the mother or others in the environment.

Organic dysfunction items

1 The mother was a chronic alcohol abuser and/or has suffered malnutrition during the pregnancy.

   The biological father was a chronic alcohol abuser before the onset of the pregnancy.

2. The child had low birth weight, was born pre-term, frequently there were birth complications.

3. The child experienced frequent hospitalizations and/or diseases. The child was kept for a long period in an incubator or in some other sensory abnormal, deprived or over stimulating, monotonous environment.

   Frequently epileptic seizures or fever convulsions, encephalitis, and early periods of ear infections, are also present.

4. Abnormal sensory-motor development. Hyper/hypo sensibility towards stimulation, abnormal reactions to touch; early hypoactivity often turns into hyperactivity at the age of 1–3. Compared to normal development the child can barely, if at all, process and react to internal sensory stimulation. There is no reaction to painful stimuli, the child eats abnormally without sensing a satiation point, doesn't sense tiredness or muscle tension, runs

around without clothes in cold weather, forgets to take off it's clothes in hot weather, does not get dizzy when swinging, has no reaction to vestibular stimulation, may be clumsy.

Often a child shows sensory extroversion (ignores internal body and skin signals and is extremely alert towards external stimuli, is thus easily distracted).

The basic body rhythms may be disturbed: sleep, eating, breathing, pulse and attention rhythms. Insufficient immune function is often seen.

The child doesn't react with normal eye contact when he is touched or caressed.

Emotional items

1. Oral fixation. The child perceives people and things as something to be consumed and forgotten.
   The contact pattern resembles early stages of development; with brief and superficial attention.
2. Absence of separation anxiety, the child lacks fear of strangers, doesn't recognize people, treats new acquaintances as old friends and is "charming and trustful". Or, the relationship is dominated by negative emotions and ambivalence.
3. Emotions are absolute and self-enforcing (joy turns into hysteria, anger into rage, etc.).
   Emotions depend on immediate stimulation, and they disappear with the stimulation source.
4. Low frustration tolerance.
   The child can't delay satisfaction and regression appears quickly when exposed to stress.
5. Absent or rigid borders towards the environment.
   The child becomes confluent with the environment, or exposes fight/flight behavior in contact.
   The child may have psychotic episodes when close emotional and physical contact is offered. Is often obsessed with fire.

Behavior and profile in test situation

1. Behavior

The child wants to score better than others. It is stimulated by new events, is easily bored by routines. It has no self-criticism or doubts.

Fight/flight/freeze behavior and attempts to manipulate you is frequent if the child is unable to solve a problem.

Answers come quickly, without any doubt, self-criticism or second thought. The child has many and uncritical associations to projective material.

He/she gives general, vague or omnipotent answers to difficult questions. The child answers questions even when ignorant. Rigid, stereotypical and infantile problem solving strategies are seen.

Applies concrete thinking in spite of abstract terminology (imitates adolescent language, shows no emotional response to "emotional" words).

Short attention span and is easily distracted by irrelevant stimuli. The child can't concentrate on any theme, task or goal for long.

The child will decline, become disorganized or refuse when presented with unstructured and vague material such as Rorschach tables, or other projective tests, and loosely defined situations or tasks. Answers will be vague and unstructured, such as "blood", "Dragon", "volcanoes" or "something burning". There will be only few answers where human figures are interpreted from the test material, and if so they will often be identified as fragmented or dismembered.

2. Test profile in WISC-R

- High-low score pattern.
- Relatively high scores in comprehension, similarities, picture completion and picture arrangement.
- Relatively low scores in arithmetic; digits span (second part), block design and coding.
- Lower scores observed in Verbal section than in Performance section. Total score is 2 points lower than normal.
- Has problems with deeper analysis, emotional/social meaning of words, inclusive terms, tasks requiring shift in strategies, seeing a problem from more than one angle, understanding proportions and connections between elements and the whole.
- Will memorize all moral rules, but is unable to comprehend and practice them in relevant situations.

In the author's study of 48 AD children, the sample was tested shortly after admission and re-tested after 18 months of intensive treatment in the institution and the on-site school. Figure 3 illustrates the result of the average sample after admission compared to the control group used throughout the study. In the re-test, the sample improved only in some practical sub-tests in spite of intensive school education indicating that the test profile may be stable over time. Later studies

CHAPTER 7

HOW CAN YOU PRACTICE MILIEU THERAPY?

Some general principles of milieu therapy

In Part One, we studied the question of why some children develop an Attachment Disorder. In the following we shall study how you can prevent this abnormal development or, if the child is older than three, how to minimize the consequences of a severe contact handicap by teaching the child compensatory coping strategies.

Milieu Therapy can be administered at many different settings. It doesn't have to be expensive to be effective. What is needed more than anything is a strong desire, efficient teamwork and a lot of patience.

The main concept of Part Two is considering the child or children you may be working with and develop a plan for treating the child/family in question by using the general framework of Milieu Therapy according to the developmental age and specific problems of the individual child. Milieu Therapy will be described in relationship to psychotherapy in the following.

What's the difference between psychotherapy and milieu therapy?

Milieu Therapy is different from psychotherapy in both means and goals. In psychotherapy, your work is always based on three premises:

1. The personal motivation. The child or the parent of the child consciously experiences some kind of suffering such as fear, neurosis or problems in social relationships. This a major motivation for entering treatment.

2. A relationship can be formed between client and therapist. A premise of successful psychotherapy is the client's ability to enter into an emotional relationship with the therapist. This ability is based on the client's childhood experience of the emotional relationship to one or both parents. It may have been difficult and problematic, but still result in object permanence in the client. As described earlier, the child must have an internal object representation that can be transferred with a relationship to the therapist.

If this object relationship is not present to some degree, the client will not feel sufficiently attached to the therapist and the emotional resistance towards attachment will surmount any underlying desire for help. If the client has a difficult relationship with you, you can help. If the client has no emotional reaction towards you, psychotherapy is meaningless.

3. In psychotherapy, you work on the psychological level by means of social contact.

In milieu therapy, you use a much broader range of theoretical angles and methods. Usually, you will work on more basic levels than the psychological approach in order to *establish the premises* of psychological and social contact. Very often, physical contact will be at first much more important than efforts to establish psychological contact.

In milieu therapy, you start with the premise that the client has few or no personal boundaries to separate him or her from the environment. Consequently "the personality" is the whole space or the entire physical room where the child is present 24 hours a day. Another premise is that you are able to influence the client emotionally only as long as you are physically present in the room since the client's ability to retain you emotionally is so minimal.

In the AD child or adult, some initial curiosity is not sufficient motivation to enable the relationship to endure the frustrations inevitable in an emotional re-organization. The AD client will find that others are "wrong" and should change their behavior, and that he or she has no reason to change. If the therapist succeeds in establishing a close emotional relationship, a very negative object representation may provoke the client to escape or to physically fight and destroy the therapist. This can occur as an intellectual hide and seek game. The AD client will imitate the behavior and opinions of the therapist and produce a "chameleon" surface. At its best, long-term psychotherapy from a stable professional will create some valuable intimacy and can be of help to the adult psychopath when the client encounters new problems due to impulsive behavior.

In psychotherapy, the emphasis is on personal and emotional development, in milieu therapy the emphasis is on compensating for the emotional handicap and its consequences. You need to be more moderate in your expectations for personal development when practicing milieu therapy. Severe AD produces a very slow rate of personality development.

By applying external structure, you will help the client to function in the present. In short, you can't reorganize the psychological structure in depth of a person after age three which means psychotherapy can generally be ruled out. After childhood long-term psychotherapy may be a useful support if there is a small chance of building a relationship with the therapist. This is especially true when the client is older than 25. Some personal maturation has often taken place leaving the client at an emotional level comparable to the teenager.

In psychotherapy, treatment will often be short-term. It relies on the client's ability to understand and retain the essence when a new experience occurs. The client will use this experience in the future, and in new situations. Internal re-organization follows the experience.

It goes without saying that since the AD child has a strongly diminished ability to learn from experience, you must repeat an experience endlessly before it is internalized. This also means that treatment is a long-term 24-hour job with the objective of gaining control of the child's environment for years.

The goals in psychotherapy focus on internal and psychological reorganization. This produces an individual who is able to function better in society.

The goals of milieu therapy are generally, apart from helping the client, to protect society and the immediate surroundings from the consequences of this handicap. It is also to help the client function as stably as possible by compensating for the emotional deficits.

On the individual level, the goal is to avoid AD development before the age of three, and to help the child organize itself to some degree of social behavior with as few as possible anti-social events.

External constancy replaces a lack of internal constancy

In milieu therapy, you focus on creating a stable and simple environment and an external motivation which comes from the therapist. If not exposed to too much change, too many people, and too little structure, the AD child or adult will ultimately be able to learn and use its often normal intelligence. If you are always present as the object, with a firm intention of teaching the child, while overcoming its resistance towards new experiences, it will be able to learn without much internal motivation which, as we now know, depends on the very early emotional bond to the mother. The daily function of the child can be greatly improved. Minimized episodes of violence, stealing, wandering will occur sometimes to a degree that resembles a very normal life. This positive effect is valuable in itself, but you should always be aware that a positive function is not the same as a lasting effective maturation in the client. In other words, positive results should not tempt you to take away your external help too quickly.

In milieu therapy, ideally, any stimulus received by the child has been filtered, focused and formed by the therapist into something the child can understand and handle, just as the mother will provide a protected environment for the relationship to the baby.

If you want the child to function (e.g. in a group with other children or in a classroom) as well as possible at any given moment, you should reduce stimulation and change. You must give the child a very calm, pre-planned and ritualized environment. If you want a child to develop, you must usually increase stimulation and lessen structure, thereby trying to enhance the child's ability to retain and transform frustration. With the AD child, function is important, and development through increased stimulation remains very moderate. There is always a delicate balance of when to introduce new challenges or tasks without disturbing function too much.

In the following paragraphs, treatment is described at the different stages following the developmental sequences described in Part One, maternal pregnancy to adulthood. At each level, important goals, methods and obstacles are defined. The major goals in milieu therapy are:

1. Reduce the number of contact-disrupting events

As demonstrated earlier, children who develop this syndrome have often experienced exposure to physical damage or intoxication to the nervous system during pregnancy, and severe complications during birth.

If you can reduce the frequency or severity of this exposure you increase the likelihood of emotional receptivity after birth. Also, if you can postpone traumatic events until the child has fully developed

skills by repeated demonstration. The objective here is that the mother performs these routines such as "changing a diaper" while receiving constant kind feedback from the case manager. The case manager should at all times ignore failure and provide positive reinforcement for even the smallest successes.

One objective of dialogues with the mother is to legalize the mother's negative feelings towards pregnancy, birth and childcare and to teach that appropriate behavior can be exercised regardless of inappropriate feelings.

In Lier's study, mothers attending the program achieved a more realistic perspective about their skills to help the baby. They were also more prone to let their baby be adopted after birth by persuasion from the now secure case manager if their skills were too few. Most important the *children born in this program did not suffer from premature births, lowered birth weight or excessive birth complications* to any greater extent than normal mothers.

Another possibility is to legally force incompetent parents to enroll the baby in a public day-care setting, where the professional day-care provider can provide attachment therapy for the baby. This intervention has been successfully used in Denmark.

Obstacles

AD mothers will often idealize motherhood until confronted with the obstacles and practical boring tasks. Psychotic mothers have extreme problems with organizing behavior, and have severe difficulties with respect to touch, intimate physical contact and coping with the natural mess and disorder that babies produce.

The case manager will take ultimate responsibility for all situations including those of failure, and will not try to be too intimate with emotional demands towards the mother. A good guideline is the question, "At what degree of emotional distance is contact optimal?" This may change with the situation, but the case manager must always be aware of not becoming too close emotionally, even when invited. The mother will often try to establish a symbiotic, extremely dependent or fighting relationship. The case manager must have regular support from the team in order to cope with strongly ambivalent feelings and too much counter-transference. Remember, the mother has often had a hostile mother herself and readily perceives the case manager as such. Sometimes, a male staff member will appear less threatening if the mother has less anxiety towards males.

The key to contact is stability, perpetual kindness and clear, simple, practical behavior demands.

Birth is generally a difficult experience, but even more so when we are talking of AD or psychotic mothers. In practice, these mothers are not skilled at interpreting internal body signals and may overlook the signs of pregnancy and beginning labor. How can you create a monitoring system that to some degree can cope with this problem?

Mothers in crisis who have less mental issues should also be considered for a similar program.

A specific problem (where systemic family therapy and/or psycho-therapy should be considered if the mother is motivated and able to benefit) is what Madsen (Madsen 1996) labels "ghosts in the nursery". In other words, the fantasies and emotions concerning motherhood in these clients are often very negative and based on the clients own early experiences in childhood. The aim of the dialogue is to help the mother revise and put into perspective her emotional reactions towards the fetus/baby. An important goal is to prevent primitive psychological defense mechanisms from overruling the bonding potential. Mechanisms such as rejection, denial (including idyllizing delusions), guilty feelings, projecting aggression onto the baby (the baby is perceived as a hostile, annoying enemy who has to be punished or annihilated) are active in all parent-child relationships, but are usually overshadowed by strong bonding impulses.

From birth to age 3: regression therapy

(Regression therapy is also used with older, less traumatized children and adults)

Even with children up to age 5, you should always start by trying to establish an emotional bond. Regression therapy is designed to do this. "Regression" means "going back", i.e. back to a non-demanding, caring mother (therapist) and baby (client) relationship. However, if this proves to be useless, milieu therapy is the next step. Milieu therapy is a form of regression therapy in a broad sense, only it is aimed at reducing the every day environment to such a small size that the child is able to function in it.

Goals

The main thing to remember is that a deprived baby at this stage has not yet entered an AD development. This means that the child will need what other babies need, only more of it. If contact has already been interrupted on many occasions or, if the child (due to organic deficits) has difficulty perceiving contact, you should use regression therapy, which in practice means providing the kind of contact that would usually only be necessary the first few months after birth until internal systems have replaced external systems. Regression therapy is non-demanding, giving, and focusing on mutual physical and visual contact. When mentioning "the mother" in the following text, a surrogate or supplementary person is included in this term. Important goals in regression therapy are:

Methods

1. Provide good nutrition

Almost all babies who have experienced deprivation will have abnormal eating patterns such as rejecting food or eating until they vomit. If the baby lacks interest and attention, stimulate by caressing it before the eating session. Give a gentle massage with a finger on the lips and around the mouth may help to elicit the sucking reflex. If the baby eats too little, provide food more frequently and in smaller portions.

2. Provide empathic tactile and vestibular stimulation

This means that the baby should receive regular sensory stimulation. If at all possible, the child should be at the mother's breast or on her body most of the time. The most dangerous sensory deprivations are kinesthetic (touch) and vestibular (movement) deprivation. Touching, sucking and skin contact is mandatory in normal emotional development and movement, such as turning, accelerating, decelerating, as happens normally when cared for.

The "Kangaroo Method", carrying the baby close to your body at all times, is an excellent tool. If the baby has to stay in an incubator for medical reasons, it should be placed on a sterilized sheepskin. This will increase the experience of being touched and the baby will gain weight 15% faster. Also, the incubator should also preferably be able to swing gently and slowly.

The baby's back and neck should be massaged gently for a few minutes every hour starting from the back of the head and moving down the neck and shoulders.

In our "visual culture" eye contact has been hailed as a starter of emotion. This is true, but before you can engage in visual contact, you must have skin and balance contact. This activates the R.A.S. system (the brain circuit regulating brain activity) and helps the baby focus the eyes on you.

An old-fashioned rocking cradle will provide a lot of vestibular stimulation with very little effort on behalf of the adult. A cradle also has the advantage that the baby receives a feedback from almost any kind of movement. Babies who have trouble relaxing or have irregular sleeping patterns will benefit immensely from a gently rocking cradle. A hammock can also be useful. A heavy "ball-eiderdown" can help if the child sleeps uncomfortably and "rotates all night" in bed. It has been developed by Danish physiotherapists and consists of plastic balls which are quite heavy (use the search word: "kugledyne" on the internet). The skin stimulation provided seems to help the baby relax and sleep more calmly.

The baby should be increasingly stimulated so gradually that it is not deprived and not over-stimulated. Stimulation should follow a stable pattern and if possible, performed by the same person. In an institution staff members should use synchronized movement patterns, tone and rate of speech and movement, bedtime rituals, etc. If possible, choose one or two case managers to avoid overwhelming the baby with multiple contact patterns.

Remember that deprived babies will often initially avoid normal body contact. This should be respected, but continuous stimulation can be replaced by more frequent contact (such as a baby massage program), until the baby has achieved a normal tolerance towards stimulation. The only exceptions from this rule are epileptic babies; epileptic seizures can be triggered by sudden stimulation. Babies suffering from Fetal Alcohol Syndrome also need to avoid over stimulation.

3. Exaggerate facial expressions and simplify personal contact

In mutual contact, you should be very expressive and clear. It's preferable to reduce other stimulation sources before making contact at the same time. When you do make contact, make sure that nobody else is in the field of vision or tries to make contact. Bring yourself into focus and clear your mind. Don't talk to the baby unless you touch it at the same time.

Deprived babies have difficulty making eye contact, and touch facilitates attention. Only one person at a time should connect with the baby, the case manager.

Exaggerate normal body language, expressions and tone of voice. You might feel a bit silly, but try to act like an enthusiastic grandmother the first time she sees the family's firstborn! When showing the baby an expression or talking to it, give the baby time to respond (up to 30 seconds), before you stimulate it again. You will be amazed when you find the slow contact-answer rhythm used by the baby.

The "Marte Meo" professional training program from Holland would be an excellent resource when working with the biological mother/parents. In this training program the interaction between mother and baby is videotaped. When reviewing the tape with the mother, the supervising case manager gives only positive feedback from those instants where natural contact and communication are successfully obtained such as eye contact, holding the baby in an appropriate close position, recognizing e.g. hunger signals correctly and responding to them, talking to the baby while changing the diaper, etc. Such successful moments may be as little as 10 seconds in 10 minutes in a dysfunctional relationship. Regardless of this, the case manager only gives positive feedback when the mother succeeds in displaying empathic and appropriate behavior. The professional caretaker or foster parent can also benefit from the attachment behavior methods taught in this program.

4. Support regularity of body rhythms

Babies suffering from organic dysfunction and deprivation will have irregular sleeping, eating, attention and EEG-patterns. Physical contact (such as being wrapped in a soft cloth) will always have a stabilizing effect. The baby should be conditioned to consistent patterns by external regularity. Make a schedule for the day which includes eating, sleeping and bathing and follow it as closely as possible. Don't expect the baby to adjust easily to this schedule; you must be flexible and patient, respecting the individual contact pattern of the baby.

5. Protect the baby from infections

Deprivation causes lowered immune system function. The baby should be protected more than usually against disease by means of vaccinations and avoid contact with children who have more serious infectious diseases.

6. Adjust the baby's stress level in order to avoid immune system problems

Again, the importance of touch and vestibular stimulation is very important to balance the activity of the immune system. If the baby has ear infections or is easily sick, use baby massage as a supplement to medical treatment. If the baby has a rash, asthma, allergies or juvenile arthritis, the same should be done. In a study by Field et al. (1997), a group of children with juvenile rheumatoid arthritis received massage from parents 15 minutes two times a day. A control group received relaxation therapy without touch. Measured by Cortisol level, an indicator for stress level, stress almost immediately decreased in those receiving massage and the children, parents and physician reported a decrease in pain, both in incidence frequency and severity of attacks.

7. Use a "Baby's Diary" and video-tapes

A good idea is to have a "Baby's Diary" which contains your basic schedule and the baby's daily reactions and responses to contact. In the diary, you should also note how long the baby is able to stay in contact with you. This can be supplemented with videotapes. Often the baby will progress slowly in its development, and the diary and tapes are a support to you as you will see even minor improvements and changes.

Try to describe or tape the same situations for comparison such as, "changing a diaper", the morning meal or being put to bed. When the child is old enough to understand, let it "help" you fill out the diary, starting with incidents that just happened and gradually covering the whole day.

Older children should have a "history book" containing data about themselves and if possible, data about parents. Both diary and history book serve the purpose of supporting the fragile sense of identity in the child.

Example from an adoptive family:

Ann was two years old when we received her. Her mother was a schizo-phrenic woman. Ann ate whatever she would get, mostly soda pops and whatever her mother would leave for her. Her skin was dry and wrinkled; she was malnourished and skinny, weighing 15% less than normal. Her eyes seemed big, partly because her head was smaller than normal for her age. She was not able to focus well visually; she took no initiative to make contact and looked away when we tried to speak to her.
Ann's muscles were underdeveloped, and she could not walk or talk. She would scream or whimper when stimulated and only became active when

offered milk in a bottle. She would then suckle too much too quickly and often vomit. We soon learned that we had to decide when she could eat, and how much. She would be quite desperate when we took the bottle away until she learned that it would return quickly. Her lip and tongue muscles were weak.

We started by wrapping her in a soft cloth and carrying her around for a few minutes. After a week we started massaging her back, arms and hands while she was lying on the stomach, four times a day, using body oils (the stomach position helps elicit postural reflexes, helping the muscles on the back and shoulders to contract and support an upright position when sitting or standing). Later, while she was on her stomach, we started circling the bottle at some distance, which forced her to practice lifting and turning her head. We would stimulate her lips and tongue with a finger before she was fed.

Ann basically experienced contact as painful and frightening and she avoided it. We had to be careful not to make sudden moves, change the light too quickly or speak loudly as she would startle and start crying. Gradually she accepted being carried in a linen cloth, and started to cling to us.

When placed in a standing position, feet on the floor, Ann would stretch her feet too much and stand on the toes. Holding her body, we would help her jump up and down on the bed or floor, this helps to inhibit the stretching reflex, and soon we could tickle her feet. Whenever she was left alone, she would engage in self-stimulation such as rocking or constantly scratching her ears. Whenever she did this, we picked her up and carried her around. When talking to her, we would embrace her. When trying to make her speak we would massage her fingers simultaneously when trying to make her utter sounds. The center of speech and the fine motor center are closely connected in the brain; stimulating one function will facilitate the other.

After two months, she would start looking at us, respond by imitating our expressions and we could use songs that included finger movements.

There was a radical change in her behavior, from an introverted, passive baby she turned into an almost too hyperactive little person. Now, she seemed determined to make up lost time. She crawled around all over the place, put everything in her mouth, opened closets and pulled things down. She still refused solid food, and protested violently when we tried to teach her how to chew. She was very frightened of water so we washed her with a wet cloth. She began to explore milk, water or anything fluid, and we could soon put her in the bathtub where she would stay and enjoy herself while slapping the water surface and screeching. The dog fascinated her, but the interest wasn't mutual. Ann would violently grab the dog and almost tear it apart. She started to talk when requesting something and we required verbal requests.

After 6 months she enjoyed her daily massage and would often hum or talk a little, while displaying a content expression you see in normal babies. She developed increasingly normal behavior, but her attention span was still very short and she showed no fear in the face of danger. She would stand on the edge of the swimming pool and just "walk" onto the water or, walk out in front of a car. This began to change when one day she was frightened by the sound of a car alarm that started unexpectedly when she stood next to it. She started crying and clinging to me. This was one of my happiest days. At the age five, she was still a very small girl, and one to two years delayed in social development. She was permitted to stay in the public school class until age seven. Today she is fairly normal, but needs to know at all times, who is in charge. If there is too much activity she looses attention and becomes restless. Ann is always afraid when we go out or have a babysitter. She has to be told in advance what is going to happen.

Obstacles

If at all possible, let the child approach the sensory stimulation voluntarily. Be aware that low, slow levels of stimulation are more efficient in creating content and interest in the child. Start with ultra-short periods of stimulation, perhaps only for seconds.

You may want to seek consultation from a Sensory Integration therapist.

Note: the abovementioned methods can be useful for children up to age 9, although their effects are most significant before age 3.

Regression and the adoption process

At this point, a special section on adopting a child is inserted. Most adopted children are newborns or toddlers up to two years. The description will highlight some of the classical issues in the early attachment process, be it for the adoptive parents or for the professional (such as the foster parent) meeting a deprived child for the first time.

If you are interested in continuing to read about milieu therapy for the preschool child, please skip to the next chapter.

TRANSIENT BONDING PROBLEMS AND ATTACHMENT DISORDER IN ADOPTED CHILDREN

Coping with separation, transition and attachment

Part I: temporary bonding problems after AB-option and AD-option

Part II: severe deprivation before adoption Symptoms of permanent attachment disorder

Part I: transition problems when acquiring new parents

This is a rather short guide to the problems you may encounter along with the joys, when adopting another human being.

Any adopted child will encounter bonding problems – for the simple reason that the child has experienced a more or less traumatic separation from parents or other adults, friends and the environment in general. It is not unusual for the child and you experience some difficulties getting acquainted at the beginning of your relationship.

The child's reaction should be understood in the context of the *real* situation of the adopted child: first, it has been *ab*-opted (Latin for *throwing someone out of a group*) from one group, and almost at the same time it has been *ad*-opted (Latin for *inviting someone to a party*) by another group without any chance of choosing whether it wanted to join that kind of party...

Imagine being fired from your job, sent across the ocean and recruited for another job which you certainly did not apply for.

Use this rule: you have no way of knowing whether your child had attachment problems before adoption until it has been with you for quite some time. If you adopt a two year old, you must follow the development until age four in order to estimate whether there are more permanent attachment problems. This span of time is called **the transition period** in the following text. Most adopted children appear delayed when you meet them only to then race through stages of physical and mental growth. The real catch-up in development will often happen 5–6 years after adoption if the child was "old" (1–3 years) when adopted. Most adopted children find ways to handle the transition between previous and new adults, and continue their development from a safe base. There are a few exceptions to this rule, which will be addressed in part II – please read part I first anyway.

In the beginning you may be shocked when the child gladly responds to anyone you meet in public but this is natural behavior, considering that he or she simply does not know you in particular. You may also be shocked when the child displays grief and fear at your first encounter. This reaction is normal and should be welcomed, it tells you that the child feels attached to someone, has a healthy reaction towards the loss and also possesses the capability for being attached to you at a later stage. The special quality of an adopted child is not that it is adopted, but that it has lived through a difficult separation from its mother, from an orphanage or from the care of a foster family. The child is then presented with two nervous strangers.

Different reaction patterns at different developmental stages

Consider how many challenges a child must face simultaneously in the short adoption process. It must survive the loss of the known; people, places, habits and intimacy. You must meet two or more complete strangers with a strange color, smell and shape (in China, Caucasians are called "long-noses"). You must quickly adjust to temperature, food and airplanes.

These experiences are most difficult if the child has been interrupted in the middle of the normal bonding process between six months and six years. Before that age, we are programmed to adapt to new adults without much effort. When adopted after age six the child is able to adjust through language, explanations and dialogue. The spoken word has increasing emotional value from this age.

It is not surprising that most children react quite a lot during this transition. They feel grief, are afraid of the new parents (who want to see the child happy from day one) want to escape from them, become hyperactive and confused from the stress of the change, become withdrawn and half mute. They try to conform to the unspoken wishes of the adoptive parents in order to please them (wouldn't you, if you were abducted by Martians?) They often cry constantly for days or even weeks. These symptoms of crisis, since that's what they are, are the more prominent, the shorter the transition phase has been. My own adopted children had 10 minutes to say goodbye to their adults and hello to us in an unfamiliar hotel room. One of them cried desperately and would have nothing to do with us until she, from pure exhaustion, had to accept falling asleep in my arms. The second child raced around the room and practically walked on the ceiling for 3 months before he finally started to act and sleep normally.

You may wonder why these reactions made me happy. They were proof that both children reacted normally in an abnormal and stressful situation. I would have been alarmed if they had just jumped in my lap. Our older child hated teddy bears for three years after we met. This is another normal reaction. We tried to give her a teddy bear in the hotel room, anything even remotely associated with that room is a source of anguish for her.

This is a mild form of Post Traumatic Stress Disorder; any association to the hotel room elicits emotional reactions from that situation. You must remember that you are also a part of that situation. Don't impose yourself on the child with your own need for security and happiness. Let the child be until it has finished crying and wants to initiate contact with you.

Psychological defense and survival mechanisms at different stages of development

Babies and young children will sometimes, depending on the degree of shock, react with the earliest defense mechanism, they become temporarily psychotic. This expression does not mean the same as it does when labeling the adult personality function. It means that the child becomes disorganized emotionally and physically until it has recovered from the experience. This is sometimes the only way a baby can survive the burdens of stress without dying. The child may cry for hours and days, and be non-responsive of any attempts to comfort. Or, it may disorganize when fatigued; wake up during the night and cry, apparently unable to perceive that someone is trying to offer security. Another reaction is an almost catatonic state of indifference to any stimulation offered.

Your main role in these situations is to be present, protect the child from more stress and see that the child has enough to drink. The physical symptoms of stress and coping methods will be described later in detail.

One of the natural psychological defenses used by toddlers in these situations is called splitting; in order to create some order in chaos, the child divides anything into white and black, good and bad, etc. This choice shows up when the child decides that the adoptive mother is the bad one and must be avoided. She resembles the person whom the child thinks has left, the child's original mother or a staff member from the orphanage, and she must be avoided, and the father or male staff member is the good one. This will usually disappear after a while, but in the meantime the rejected person has had another blow to her self-confidence as "the lovable mother".

Jealousy and feelings of rejection and incompetence can be transferred from the child to the caretakers – a very good subject for conversation when the miracle has fallen asleep, if it does sleep at all.

Also, you may encounter Paradoxical Attachment Behavior. The loss of familiar adults triggers insecurity in the child and the adoptive parents are consequently challenged in two different ways at the same time. As a source of necessary comfort, security and care and, as a threat, because "this adult may leave me"; just like the adults it trusted have done. This makes the child alternate between approach and rejection in the same sequence of behavior. The child may hug you one minute, totally rejecting, beating, hurting and escaping from you the next. This can go on all day.

Food thank goodness is the primary source of comfort. The child may have nothing to do with you, but offer food any time without restrictions, and prove that you can be trusted in that respect.

A third survival mechanism is "the blind spot". The child will behave as if the most tempting bonding possibility did not exist, and ignore that particular person carefully as she represents the dangers of love, a possible new rejection.

The child adopted as a preschooler may have more mature defense mechanisms such as guilt, shame and conflicts of loyalty between earlier adults and adoptive parents/sisters/brothers. The preschool child has already developed the stepping stones of identity and an initial self-conscience. It is also constructing a set of tools to connect the relationship to the environment. This includes language, culturally determined behavior patterns and normative feelings and concepts.

At the preschool level, the dawning sense of identity is interwoven with a stable environment that will constantly provide affirmative feedback. At this level of development, you really can't separate yourself very well from your surroundings. Consequently, a loss of the familiar environment will often be a loss of the familiar concept of self. A major initial problem may be that the child suddenly encounters people who don't understand a word it says, not even when it asks where the bathroom is. This problem may be emphasized if the child had previous experiences of rejection. The child may react to this by feeling "wrong" or guilty when not speaking the language of the adoptive parents.

The underlying psychological mechanisms of these feelings have to do with separation. They are in fact the preschooler's normal reaction to separation and loss. A child this age will usually create an emotional interpretation of separation; "I have been rejected, because I was un-lovable, ugly, or whatever negative quality". One compensational mechanism to avoid feeling rejected is feelings of omnipotence, usually projected to the former milieu and parents "My old home was much better than this, my father was a mayor in a city, you are nobody, you don't understand me", etc. Another way of coping with rejection is false cynicism "I don't care where I am, I don't care whether you like me, I do what I want, I don't need parents". A third way is withdrawal; if you don't contact anyone, nobody can reject you again. A fourth way is to try to please and foresee any parental expectation, being afraid of failure or being utterly self-controlling. This last coping mechanism often creates a dangerous connection with the adoptive parent's fear that "something might be wrong with me as a parent". In this case, there is an unholy alliance between the child's fear of a new rejection and the parent's fear of failure. The result is adopted children who speak and walk very early, behave better than other children of the same age. But these children have an air of constant sadness or a host of psychosomatic problems because fear is the basis of their "good" behavior.

How can you convey to a child the knowledge that **low self-esteem, lack of curiosity and dependence are normal reactions to separation**? Well, one way of nurturing the preschool child's transition into the adoptive family is to be able to contain these defenses and not perceive it as a personal message to you from the child. This is difficult and requires a lot of dialogue between the adoptive parents, something that often enriches the marital relationship. Second, it is a good idea to convey to the child, in a way you find natural and comprehensible way, that these reactions are the way children cope with separation. For example, "You don't like me, and you often tell me that I should go away. You miss the people you came from, and the friends you had. You think that loving me would be betraying them. You know what, that's okay with me! You see, I know that when a child is adopted, this child feels thrown away and not worth anything. All children feel that way when someone leaves. That's also okay with me. I like you, and I would be proud if you would be my son/daughter. I like you so much you don't have to like me. I know how sad you are, with us, you can be sad as long as you like. Some day, I look forward to hearing about your sadness".

This kind of open conversation will make it easier for the child to understand negative, forbidden feelings about you which are produced by the separation.

As an adoptive parent you yourself also carry the unconscious burdens of rejection experiences from your own life. Don't make them the child's problem by overriding defense mechanisms with insisting and hasty illusions of love. Ask yourself if you are caressing the child because you are afraid of being rejected or because you and the child both find caressing a natural thing to do right now. Be present, be aware, be kind, be receptive, but let the child always take the first step. Look at it this way, no matter what you do only one person can choose to accept you as a parent. Talk to other adoptive parents or an independent therapist, not only about the child, but about your own reactions when being rejected by the child.

Physical stress symptoms in the transition period

There are a number of physical stress symptoms in the recently adopted child.

Most prominent are mild eating disorder symptoms. The child refuses to eat or eats only to feel secure. Problems with digestion are often seen (diarrhea, colic and bladder and feces control).

Be certain that the child has enough to drink. A period without food is not harmful, unless the child is already malnourished. If this is the case, see a doctor immediately. Sleep disturbances and night terrors are common even though the child may seem unaffected in the daytime.

Some stress problems can be helped by using baby massage, or carrying the child close to your body most of the time. Bathing together is also a good activity for soothing and becoming acquainted. Don't let your efforts be deterred if the child refuses physical contact in the beginning and make sure you present contact respectfully and insisting. Use less threatening situations such as hugging in a towel after a bath or a little massage to the neck and back at bedtime. Don't touch the front of the body; this will elicit more defense reactions than touching the back and neck. Take your time and do it in a calm, gentle way.

Regression is necessary

Regression is another normal reaction after adoption. The child literally takes a step backwards in development in order to survive the strains. A child can learn a lot of behavior patterns out of pure fear of being rejected. It is a good idea to show the child that you can control your fear of abnormality and your wish for a "normal" child developing at "normal" rate. You may offer it a bottle of milk, let it wear a diaper again, show joy when the child is at ease instead of when it acquires a new skill.

It is generally a good idea to offer the child the kind of care it would need if it were only half its own age.

With the first adopted child, it is difficult not to worry too much in the beginning and let the child be who it is. Introduce stable habits and familiar surroundings to help the child recognize people, actions and places as easily as possible. Wait to visit family and new places for the first few weeks.

You should talk to your spouse about what the child did or said and also about your own fears, separation experiences from your own childhood and what anxieties can make you too goal oriented on behalf of the child.

The crisis of the adoptive parents

It is important to realize that you yourselves experience a crisis when you have the first adopted child. Many adoptive couples find that the years of waiting, the professional books and the great expectations make the meeting with the child so significant that the spouses are of little help to each other. Feelings of grief from not having a biological child of your own may emerge again. Be sure that both of you have someone else to talk to. What its like to be a mother (and how foolish adoptive fathers are) or a father (and how foolish adoptive mothers are). Accept that both parties need someone neutral to talk to. Receiving help from others is not a threat to marital loyalty, unless you hide it from each other. You must be patient with yourself and your spouse in this difficult phase of becoming a family. It is a good idea to form a group with other adoptive parents. This group can also become an important emotional base for the children involved. When they are teenagers, they can share how foolish adoptive parents are, while the parents share how difficult adopted teenagers are.

The first year after adoption, the parents must adjust to a child they haven't known from birth and must also find ways of organizing a family system as parents. This is quite a sudden change compared to the course of a normal birth. This is probably why adoptive families who receive counseling in the first year have more secure adoptive children than those who don't have access to this support (Juffer 1997).

Part II: children with permanent attachment disorder

A small group of adopted children will have major problems when the attachment process should take place. Some children are severely deprived and apparently without contact abilities when received in their new surroundings. Some recover and attach and a few percent display major problems. Whether a child suffers from AD can only be determined at age 5. So, you have to be patient. You should let professionals make the diagnosis whenever possible. About 10% of all adopted children in Denmark receive help later in school because of severe learning disabilities and conduct problems. In general, (remember that statistics are invalid when concerning just one child!) post-adoption studies show that the number and severity of problems increases with age at the time of adoption.

The subject of AD is described in detail elsewhere in this book, but I shall comment on how AD appears in adopted children. A general lack of care is difficult to separate from severe AD. Generally, to predict possible AD it is more important to know the child's environment from conception to age three, rather than their current condition.

First, adopted children who develop AD are usually older than one when adopted. They may have had an even longer period of neglect and other traumatic experiences before the adoption. When adopted the child is often past the most important attachment period (0–3 years).

If children have a physical handicap, chances are greater they may also have been exposed to violence or neglect, especially in cultures where weakened children have been rejected by family or state (e.g. Romania, Bulgaria). The sex may also play a cultural role, boys can be favored (e.g. China). A general famine or lack of nutrition can also cause damage to brain development.

Second, boys are more vulnerable to stress and neglect, 3 out 4 with AD diagnosis are boys.

You should remember that statistics do not apply to individuals. If you are offered a boy, look at the boy in question, and not the statistics.

Third, you can gain insight about the emotional capacity of the child by looking at the child's health history. If the mother was a drug abuser or an alcoholic, chances are greater for minor brain damage and later problems with impulse control, concentration and aggression. If there were birth complications, premature birth or low birth weight, this adds to the possibility of minor brain damage. If the mother was a psychiatric patient or has moved often and had many promiscuous relationships, this may be an indicator of her lack of ability to care for the child. However, a normal person can be driven into prostitution and yet been able to provide basic childcare. Also, you can look to see if another caretaker has been able to take over the attachment process. This may be a family member, staff in an orphanage or a foster family. You can determine how many times this child has been given another caregiver. The more people, the smaller the chance the attachment process has succeeded.

Notice whether staff or other caregivers seem to generally have a respectful and loving attitude towards the children in their care, or if they appear to have low self-esteem and care for the children in a detached routine manner without personal contact with each child. Is there a system where a few people are responsible for a group of children or random shifts?

The most detrimental impact on the development of attachment is found when all of the negative stress factors mentioned above appear in the early life of a child. This will make it more likely that the child will have severe problems in the attachment process and is at risk for developing AD.

A case from my practice:

Two sisters are adopted from an Eastern Europe country, aged five and six. They are never at ease, and often commit violent acts towards other children. At age nine and ten, they experience premature start of menses. At age ten and eleven, their conduct problems have reached a level, where they are suspended from their third school. They are sent to a therapeutic center where the staff is eagerly discussing the subject of sexual abuse, which has become a media event. After a week, both girls claim that their adoptive father has abused them sexually through childhood, confirmed by the therapeutic center, and he is sent to trial. During this, the girls' testimony proves extremely inconsistent and contradictory, and they cling to repeating the term "sexual abuse". They often laugh, shout and giggle, enjoy being the center of attention and show no signs of trauma during the trial. The charges are dropped, and a week later they claim the same charges against a staff member at the center. The sisters frequently run away and eventually the therapeutic center states that the girls are not motivated for treatment, and do not understand that they have a problem. The adoptive parents have felt stigmatized by professional and move to another area. The girls are now in their home only when they follow a set of "parole agreements" set up by me, the girls and the parents.

This is a severe case of AD. At the other end of the scale, "Jaime's" case may illustrate mild AD symptoms:

Jaime was adopted at age two from a South American foster family who found him in the street when he was approximately six months old. Today, Jaime is ten. He has problems with concentration and the ability to stay on task. Without constant support he only does what he wants to do. He will sometimes lie if it is more convenient, and he is unable to foresee that the truth will surface in a few minutes or hours. He is extremely charming, articulate and liked by new people who do not understand why his adoptive parents keep saying that he has problems. He frequently talks to people on the street. Jamie often fantasizes about what he will do when he grows up, but the means to create the possibilities are of little interest to him. He does not run away or steal, and at first glance only appears to be somewhat immature. However, his sexual activities and games often cross the line of what other children and their parents will accept. He is popular in school and good at sports. He always makes new friends who disappear after a few weeks. He probably won't be able to take responsibility for his own life, and his parents worry about his adulthood and who will look after him, since they themselves are rather old.

End of Adoption Section

CHAPTER 9

MILIEU THERAPY FOR THE PRESCHOOL CHILD

Milieu therapy for the preschool child

Between ages 3–6 it is easier to determine if the child has succeeded in attaching to a parental figure. If not, it becomes increasingly evident that other children mature at a faster rate. The problem will now be the gap between age in years and age in emotional development. Other children will often be aware of this and choose not to be with the AD child. The child may have a lot of temporary friends, but no lasting relationships. The child in its turn will try to cope with social demands by imitating behavior and phrases it does not really understand, or by having temper tantrums. The relationship to all adults will also often be compromised. The initial "charming" behavior of the child is misinterpreted as open-mindedness and trust, only to be followed by disbelief when the child proves how immature it really is.

The typical observations from preschool and kindergarten will be:

The professional's observations

- The child will swiftly change roles according to the situation.
- The child will blame other children or adults for its own actions.
- The child can "say the right things" – but not stick to an agreement.
- The child reacts strongly when exposed to changes or new situations.
- The child can only function well when alone with an adult.
- Both positive and negative experiences end up in conflict.
- Trust and positive situations will be sabotaged by the child.
- The child shows no signs of guilt, second thoughts, fear.

Behavior in child groups

- The child is obsessed with control issues (submission/dominance).
- The child does not respect the social, sexual and personal limits of others.
- The child insists on making its own rules in social games.
- The child feels persecuted by others, when the reverse is the case.
- The child will discuss and object to demands and rules – endlessly.
- The child is unable to see itself as a group member ("they/I" instead of "we").
- The group must be monitored constantly and is unable to work.

Behavior when learning or exercising

- The child does not learn from experience.
- The child can learn by memorization, but not reorganize knowledge in new patterns.
- The child can only see differences, but not common traits or properties.
- The child thinks in absolute and concrete terms.
- The child has a short attention span.
- The child avoids repetition and routine work, is restless and prefers anything new.
- The child cannot evaluate its own work critically.

The essence of these observations is listing the problems of a very immature child. The observations should be prominent when the child is compared to other children of the same age. This list is also applicable when observing the older AD child and the juvenile, since we are talking about a chronic arrest in development.

Goals

To balance social demands with the child's capacities. To teach the child to do what you ask it to do. Make the world "small" enough to be comprehensible. Focus on behavioral demands, not on emotional demands. Teach others how to behave with the AD child. Create an organized, kind and simple structure for social contact.

- **A low degree of flexibility and complexity in processing**
  emotionally: is stubborn, can't perceive an argument or a feeling.
  Is easily confused when adult feelings are mixed or have a low
  degree of intensity. Cannot modify an attitude.
  cognitively: can only work when step-by-step methods are used. Is
  confused by relative arguments, is confused when a task contains
  more than one variable or includes interdependent variables.
  Problems understanding grammar.

The abovementioned faculties are the prerequisites for "learning how
to learn" and at the same time they constitute a list of lacking or
immature functions in the deprived or relationship-disturbed child. It
is also a list of where to focus your work: before starting to learn how
to read or write, the child must learn how to learn! After one year, it
is a better result if the child can concentrate for 60 seconds instead of
the initial 5 seconds on a subject, than having learned all the letters
of the alphabet by heart. It is a far better result that the child can
reverse a process (like counting backwards) than being able to count
to a hundred.

This means that most of what the teacher has learned about
normal children has less value when teaching of the AD child.
Concepts such as "Children are happy, trustful, self-regulating individuals, they have personal competence, should make personal
choices, should experience new things every day, should have close
social and emotional relationships, learn how to discuss, negotiate
and debate", etc. etc. Dismiss all this, at least for the first two years
in class. Most of these concepts are true with the child who enters
school with a healthy bonding experience, but they exceed the
competences of the AD child. In fact these concepts create chaos in
the AD child and elicit primitive defense mechanisms, fight/flight
behavior or withdrawal.

When you are with an AD child, you will inevitably have an
increasing feeling of becoming distracted – since that's the child's
problem. You start thinking; "Where were we? – Where was I? – What
was I just planning? – What time is it? – Why did I take this job?"

How to find the subject in a sentence …

At a seminar, a teacher summed up the essence of working with the
AD child's fragile object relationship. She asked: "How can I teach
him grammar? He has no awareness of himself, so he doesn't know
where to find the subject in a sentence, where to find the object,

where to find anything". After some discussion of this important statement, we decided that he should learn grammar by standing in the open, facing the standing teacher. Then, he would practice saying: "**I** stand here, so **I**'m the **subject** – **you** stand there, so **you** are the **object**, now I **walk** over to you, so "walk' is the **verb**". That helped him, at age 10!

The teacher as the relationship organizer or: stop giving him motorbikes – build a cradle!

Virtually all new teachers overestimate the abilities of the AD child by unconsciously assuming the presence of basic functions (such as conscience, attachment to the teacher, awareness of oneself, guilt and social empathy). This overestimation stems in part from the pseudo-social surface developed by the child to survive, an apparent charm and spontaneity, so difficult to recognize as being simple immaturity, and in part from the unconscious use of your own childhood attachment process as a general frame of reference for your expectations.

It is very confusing to realize that emotional and intellectual developments are quite separate processes. The neurological foundations for emotional response are developed from birth to age three, whereas the cortical intellectual development has it's heyday from age $1\frac{1}{2}$ to approximately age 17. Only when you are close to the AD child do you realize that the elaborate cognitive phrases are imitations of adult language. The child can willingly repeat any social and moral rule or norm – but cannot practice even the simplest one. Often, you will be deeply disappointed after an initial period of optimism, when you discover that the child is unable to respond to most of your professional approaches.

The primary element in teaching is to create a meaningful relationship, **to be a clear object to the child** – regardless of the contents of the matter you want to convey. In the case of the AD child, you may **divide the age by three or four**, in order to find the pattern of relating in a comprehensible way. How do you react properly, when a two-year old has a fit of rage? How long will you let a two year old out of sight and expect him to be calm and content? How much would you expect him to understand the practical consequences of your moral standards?

This may be how you should react to the 10–14 year old AD child. This is especially true in areas where emotion is evoked. In other situations of a more cognitive and factual character, you may address the same child as a normal ten year old.

Children with a fragile or inconsistent primary object relationship tend to survive through **regression**. When stressed, they easily return to the emotional internal organization of the baby. That includes fight/flight behavior, avoiding demands, terminating eye contact, trying to change the environment instead of adjusting itself to circumstances.

You must be able to respond properly to regression by examining how your behavior elicited defense mechanisms, and by responding at the same level as the child has (temporarily) regressed. Your behavior should be **complementary**: if the child is "age two" right now respond to that age. If the child is "age five" right now respond appropriately.

It is generally a good idea to study developmental psychology, emotional as well as cognitive, in order to be able to recognize and respond to behavior from different developmental stages. Your own prior experiences with toddlers and babies are invaluable also.

The following phase descriptions are a general guide to "organize the disorganized" classroom environment of the AD child. You must fill in the gaps with your imagination and flexible professional creativity – these are only suggestions for your practice. It is important that you grasp the meaning of the suggested structure and adapt it to your own professional practice. The suggestions are based on what was mentioned earlier in this text: namely that the AD child has major problems due to an insufficient ability to organize the emotional and perceptional field. This in turn stems from problems when perceiving the original object, the parent, especially when the background changes. In milieu settings, you keep the background stable and ritualized.

There is no time limit attached to each phase. It is your own judgment that will tell you when to move to the next step. You may also prepare yourself for moving *down* each time the child is disturbed by events outside your control, such as, "Mum tried to kill herself again – for the 43rd time this year".

Being a clear object to the child

Make yourself and your environment **recognizable** to the child by using rituals, re-occurring situations and stable background settings. Make yourself **inevitable** by your requesting something the child can perform. Make yourself **positive** by offering something the child desires, and can obtain if meeting your request. Make yourself a **secure** base by always being present, realistic, non-blaming, guiding **patient**ly. Create only **one focus** or work with one subject at a time.

The time span of the child **is very limited**, you can only perceive time for as long as you can sustain an emotion, and that's not very long in the AD child. It is very important that you initially only **use the present tense**, only refer to things and people actually present and that you don't talk about "yesterday" or "tomorrow". If you talk about the future, only use the immediate future: "**Now** we are going to ..., now I will ..., now you shall ...". The same goes for the past.

Take full responsibility

Being responsible towards an AD child means taking all responsibility for what happens, for setting the right goals and for any conflict.

Whatever goes wrong, there is only one cause of failure, and that's you (this is what it means to be a container for the child's problems). When something goes wrong, you simply and calmly state, "That's my fault, this task was too difficult for you – that's why you didn't learn it like I said you would" or "Too bad you set the house on fire that's because I was away from you for 5 minutes – that was 3 minutes too long!" or "You tried to stab him with a pencil – I wasn't fast enough to stop you before you even took it up – next time I'll do better". Easy and true, once you get used to it. Notice that you never say you are sorry or excuse what you did, you state what you did, and how it wasn't sufficient to fulfill your total responsibility for all that happens in the classroom. No more, no less.

Teaching in phase I: establishing the object and the background

It's a good idea to teach the children to wait outside the classroom, until you arrive. The psychological message is that the world begins when the teacher comes. It also places the initiative where it should be: with you. If you think this is too authoritarian, you must find other ways to bring yourself into the emotional focus from the start.

The first hour is the most important, and your willingness to take responsibility for all that goes on in the classroom is imperative. Don't say, "Hello". **State your name** and why you are here. Tell the child who you are, why someone can trust you, what you want from each child, and what behavior you expect from the children. Never mention what you do not want or like, it will happen immediately.

Tell the child what it will learn, because **you** have decided it is a good thing to learn (never make the child responsible in the start). If the child expresses doubts about your goals, your answer is that she or he shouldn't worry, since children don't have to be able to learn, you, the teacher, can help them learn anyway.

If anybody has trouble learning, **he or she will come to you** or you to him (as opposed to asking other children). If you have a class of 6, think of it as 6 "parent-child" relationships, not as "a teacher and the group".

Next, tell the children about **the room** they are in. Don't tell them anything about any other room until they are physically present in that room. Only **use the present tense**. What the room is used for, size and shape, what you use for sitting, what the room looks like and the purpose of different items. Only talk about things and matters you want the child to have as future points of attention. Then, talk about the materials and their purpose in the room: this is a pencil, you use it for writing and hold it like this, this is your bag you use it for this and treat it like that, you always put it there, etc.

Avoid having objects in the room if they don't serve a specific, accounted-for purpose. Make a clear indication as to when the short lesson starts and ends, and how to leave the classroom (e.g. you leave first and help the children get their coats outside the classroom before you escort them to the secluded playground). Always use the same room, have the children sit in the same place; don't move anything around from day to day. Don't let anyone, adult or child, leave or enter the classroom without your permission. Nobody can "pop in with just a short message" while you are teaching, they must knock and wait for your permission to enter, and address only you. Your cell phone and intercom are off.

Please remember:

- Never bargain.
- Never discuss.
- Decide!

The next day, do the same thing all over again in the same way. Gradually during the first weeks, ask the children to help you remember ("Oh, how am I to use this schoolbag??").

It may be necessary to follow this procedure for weeks, sometimes for years if the child is severely handicapped.

Using multi-sensory impacts for conceptualization

When you have enough automatic behavior patterns to ensure a reasonably quiet class, you can start introducing academics into your teaching. Show the children in your movement pattern that all teaching is a process between the teacher and the individual child. Give them individual tasks according to their level of comprehension. Start requesting skills that you are absolutely certain the child is already capable of doing.

Use sensory-motor methods of teaching: don't talk about the book, let the child hold, see, touch the book also. Use teaching tools that incorporate many senses: you can touch a wooden letter, smell it, hear it knock, move it, put it in a row with other letters, etc. Don't explain grammar in words, stand on the floor and say:' "I stand **here**, so I am the **subject** – **you** stand **there**, so you are the **object** – I **walk** over to you that's the ..." as mentioned previously. These very concrete ways of learning help the child conceptualize in depth. Any concept is founded on a perception and a set of sensory experiences. The AD child does not come with a broad range of sensory experiences, or ideas about how to order and arrange them into concepts.

Encourage "thinking aloud", not too loud, when working on a problem. That's how young children learn to think. Thinking aloud helps the child organize problem solving. "Tell yourself what to do and how to do it". The child says: "First I take out my pencil, then I put the paper in front of me, then I ..."

You **present a task** to the child by taking full responsibility and motivation yourself. The child probably has a very negative attitude concerning its own ability to learn, has been rejected by several schools and adults, etc. You say: "**I** have decided that today you will learn how to write two different letters. You don't have to think you can do it and you don't have to like to do it. Now I'll write down what I decided you will learn today". At the end of the day, you say, "You see the note I made this morning? Now you can write two letters, so I put the note in this box (things learned). Tomorrow, I'll give you another task. We have two boxes here, things **I** decided you will learn, and things **I** decided you did learn".

A method for developing social self-awareness in the child

Phase I: mapping abnormal behavior patterns

Use the first month in class for *observing all specific behavior problems of each child* and notice how each child relates or avoids relating to you.

Do a ten-minute observation or better yet, have a colleague do it for you while you teach. Note any behavior that your experience tells you is not normal; either something the child does, like screaming or being violent to others, etc. or, the *way* it is done, banging up the door, running through the room, shouting loud, throwing the school-bag in a corner, interrupting a conversation, etc. Only note behavior: He does this, then this, etc.

Phase I is completed when you have a clear notion of simple abnormal behavior patterns produced by each child.

Phase II: directing attention towards patterns

The AD child has very little awareness of itself, its behavior patterns, and its impact on the surroundings. The most contact deprived children will have no self-awareness at all, the less deprived will be so insecure that they constantly seek external confirmation of their existence, calling for attention incessantly. This, combined with motor impulsivity, is the main reason for most of their conduct problems.

At the end of the day, create short sessions where the children can study themselves in mirrors or view and comment on short video sessions taken during the day. You may direct the children's attention to recurring behavior patterns, but don't praise or scold any behavior; just help the child recognize how it behaves during the day, for example, how it eats if this is a problematic behavior. When the behavior reoccurs in the classroom, you can refer to the video experience in order to help the child separate itself from the situation. You may give a lot of instant neutral feedback when you observe a behavior pattern, or you may discuss narcissistic problems in short sessions, such as: "Do I disappear or die if no-one is looking at me?" In later sessions, you may use group feedback among the children, if you feel that the children are now able to describe each other's behavior without too much aggression.

Phase III: recognizing behavior patterns

When you have established a stable learning routine and a certain level of self-conscience, it is time to instigate the understanding phase, that is, helping the child understand why it has difficulty learning.

First, you return to your initial observations of each child's behavior problems.

You use this list to create a short lecture in class, starting with some general statements:

1. Babies who were not touched very much, were hungry, were beaten; were separated because of illness, etc. have problems when they grow older. All parents want to care for their new babies, but some do not have the strength, do not feel well enough, are too angry, or don't know how to care for a baby, some are sick. Not all parents can care for their babies in a good way even though they want to. No one is to blame, not the child, or the parents. Everybody tries the best they can. Some children had many problems when they were babies, and did not get much help. Nobody showed them what to do. This is why we are here in this class; to learn what to do.
   The babies who were in need **all do the same things** when they grow older.

2. These things are (use your initial observations):
   – Running away and fighting.
   – Not being able to listen to what grown-ups say.
   – Being distracted or can't concentrate.
   – Wanting to hurt other children or destroy things.
   – Arguing about anything the teacher says.
   – Always wanting to be somewhere else or talking to someone else.
   – Thinking you'll not be noticed when the teacher looks at someone else.
   – Feeling worthless.
   – Being suspicious.
   – Doing anything so the grown-up will watch you.
   – Having fits of rage for no reason.
   – Hating other children or adults.

And anything else you have seen in the classroom. You can write or illustrate the list or use other approaches, depending on the age of the children.

Babies are smart; they always do the best they can. If someone hits you, you hit back, if nobody touches you, or you bang your head onto the wall or rock all the time. That's the smartest thing the baby can do. If living was difficult for the baby, it will *continue* doing what was the smartest thing to do *even* if it grows older.

3. How to learn anyway.
   State that no child is responsible for the problems mentioned above and that the child can learn how to make even smarter ways of behaving – it does not have to love, only to learn how to behave together with the teacher and the class.

It is imperative that you present the abovementioned behaviors for what they are: *normal* reactions to early lack of attachment and therefore the best the baby could do. Do this in a way that is not overly emotional, just kind and matter-of-fact, this is how it is. You should emphasize that coping with "old behaviors" is a simple learning process, and that the purpose of this class is to learn about social behavior. The outcome will be that the child can behave like other children of the same age, and some day can be rid of annoying adult control.

The aim of this phase is to provide enough self-conscience to make the child more self-adjusting in class. *Phase IV is completed when each child recognizes and knows some of its own behavior patterns* and can say: "I do this or that" or "I do it in this way". Do not proceed until this goal has been achieved. Remember: the AD child is not aware of itself and its impact on the environment to any normal extent. The most important goal is to make the child realize this impact.

Phase IV: using the "behavior joystick".
Exercise variations of basic baby behavior patterns

If you can make the child create *any* variation of a behavior pattern, the behavior is no longer impulsive; it is controlled by the child itself. The purpose of Phase V is to use *variation* as a way to controlling your own behavior. As soon as you are able to perform a variation of a pattern; it will no longer be an unconscious impulse-driven act. A planned and executed variation in itself (however incomplete) will mean that the goal of controlled behavior is being achieved.

All behavior consists of two variables: intensity and speed.

Take one of the behavior patterns (simple, short actions from the observation list, such as "banging on the door, running through the room, interrupting a conversation"). Do not try to change the pattern in any way, show accept.

Let one child at a time perform that behavior while the others form a "panel". Only this time the child must perform that behavior *according to instruction,* such as:

1. Can you do it twice as fast?
2. Can you do it in three times as fast?
3. Can you do it in slow motion, how slow can you do it?
4. Can you shout twice as loud?
5. Can you whisper all the way?
6. Can you do it backwards (start where you interrupt a conversation)?
7. Can you throw your bag twice as fast?
8. How slowly can you throw the bag?

The children can take turns acting out each example.

You can also use modification of language stereotypes such as "You moron", or any other aspect of behavior. Don't try to change the exact phrase, only the way it is expressed. Show that you are only interested in the way it is done, not the contents.

Show approval whenever variation is achieved and ignore failures.

You can work in the same way with enhancing frustration tolerance. Take a bag of small candies and ask the children to stand in line in front of you. Tell them that the first person will get one candy; the second will get two, the third in line three, etc. Or put two candies on a table, you stand with the child at the opposite end of the room and give the instruction that whoever is *the last* to get to the table will get *both* candies. Think of more ways to practice frustration tolerance.

At the end of each session, say that today the children proved again that you can change behavior. It is possible and was proved in this session: you can do something in different ways.

At this point, do not make any demands for behavior change outside these lessons.

Before you continue; check that all children have tried and are aware that they can create variations in behavior.

Phase V: the "class lab for alternative behavior"

Instead of forbidding or interrupting negative behavior, the exercises are designed for developing more mature patterns from the original (baby) ones. Now make a lab, where the children can give suggestions for adding quality to behavior that has a better chance of creating accept in others and achieving goals.

For a start, tell the children that the wise baby always wanted something relevant, when it started crying or beating or screaming: it may have been hungry or may have wanted attention. That we are now to work with: *ways of getting what you want*. And how do you make others give you what you want? If you do it right, you will get what you need. If not, people will scold or reject you. So how do you behave to get what you want?

An example: Sit in a circle and select one familiar, generally unacceptable behavior pattern that the children can work on improving. A child performs it – then you have a brief group discussion. "What else can you do here? Can it be done in another way? Suggestions, please" With each suggestion, the behavior is acted out with the new modification. After two or three modifications introduce another discussion; "How will others respond to this way?". Then take another pattern and run it through the modification mill, and so forth. An adult can play "the counterpart" and give feedback on the modified pattern. At the end of each session, have the children discuss: "Would it be okay for you, if someone did it this way/using those words towards you?"

You are the final judge of whether a method of behavior will lead to the desired outcome, acceptance and gratification. You may use a performance scale from 1–10 and give little prizes for a certain number of points.

Remember that success is connected with anxiety in the child, and as performance improves, defense mechanisms will be activated (sabotage, diversion maneuvers, conflict). Explain this as another "wise guy move from the baby inside". Respond with the attitude "We (the teachers) know that you will reach this goal (improved behavior patterns), so we will continue".

When the children have designed and performed new behavior patterns for a while, can cooperate on making new patterns as a matter of routine, Phase V is completed.

Phase VI: transferring the lab to the classroom

At this point you may choose some of the new behavior patterns and make incorporate them into your classroom rules. Only take a few and point out in what situations they are to be used.

If a child comes running into class, slamming the door, you can now say "Eric, would you please do that in slow motion, and when you reach us, wait until I have finished talking to Janet. Just stand here with us".

In sessions you teach how the new behavior patterns can be used in the class (not outside the classroom yet). Control the discussions by taking suggestions and make the choices of behavior patterns yourself. Discuss the problems children have when performing the new behaviors, and ask for suggestions to overcome them. In real classroom situations, you can say "Stop! Let's try that again" if someone fails and needs help.

Phase VII: teaching others what we do in class

The class invites guests (other children, other teachers) and tells them why they are in this special class, what the children in this class are working on, what they were unable to do when they started, and what they can do now. The children may instruct the guests in performing some of the exercises.

At this point, for short periods of time, you may start sending children out of class in pairs to perform a modified behavior sequence (e.g. "walk around in the schoolyard in a calm way").

Ethics

Many teachers will refrain from being direct when dealing with Attachment Disorder. However, it is my personal ethical opinion that children who are enrolled in a special school setting have a funda- mental right to know why their parents or caretakers have placed them there. They have a right to honest information about the attachment problems that they have to live with every day. Besides, the chance of getting their cooperation improves if they know that people think they have problems and demonstrate strategies to resolve them. If you suffered from some disease or problem, wouldn't you appreciate that people in your environment acknowledged it, talked about it, and gave you precise and honest information?

Finally, it is my experience that AD children already have a vague and fragmented idea about their own reaction patterns and behavior problems. However, they don't know what to do about them and they don't encounter adults who dare talk about them. They have been corrected and talked to many times when things have gotten out of hand, but someone never really talked to them about why and what behavior problems they have in a factual and direct manner.

How do we start?

You will of course ask yourself "Can I/we work in this way?" If you have tried regular educational approaches, it probably hasn't worked. Is a chaotic classroom ethical? It is my experience that you don't have to be a trained therapist in order to use this teaching approach. Freud stated that the best therapists are never psychologist, but laymen – since they have another professional practice which they can integrate into their therapy.

The task of the teacher is to teach and qualify knowledge in the child, only in AD children, teaching starts from the bottom with learning how to learn.

You must of course discuss this method with your colleagues and anyone else involved. Ask people to read this information in order to find common guidelines for introducing this approach.

Summary: important goals/success criteria

1. The child has learned to focus attention on you (look at you and listen), to receive behavior instruction and perform it, and to receive your help with minimal resistance and without fight/ flight behavior. This is usually after an initial series of confrontations where the child discovers that you mean whatever you say, and that you only present reasonable – but unavoidable – requests.
2. The child perceives you as being impossible to move, destroy, distract, con or escape from. In short, you can be trusted. You are calm and kind and taking responsibility for anything that goes wrong.
3. You have found the appropriate level where the child can learn. You have a calm and realistic approach to the child, knowing that development is delayed, and the maturity age is approximately one third of the chronological age.
   You can request work in class, and the child attempts to comply.
4. You have accepted that the child can learn by memorization, but does not understand much of the social and emotional meaning of what is learned (a behavior sequence, a text, a social rule, etc.).
5. The child has acquired knowledge about how early deprivation/ violence affects its present behavior and problems. The child is aware that these causes are no excuse for current misconduct, rather, it is a challenge to learn new social coping strategies. Normal behavior can be learned.

6. The child knows that you are always confronting behavior problems quickly kindly and consequently. Mainly, anticipate problems and act before they escalate.
7. When deciding the level of teaching for each child, you "peel onions", i.e. you find the child's real level of knowledge and start just below that level.

It is always up to your judgment, when the class will be ready to move from one phase to another. Sometimes you must work for months in one phase, sometimes things go more smoothly. If the children have too much difficulty, go one step backwards.

Better to be too slow than too quick. There are three ways to help AD children; patience, patience and patience. Well, perhaps four?

Necessary organization

The name of the class should be factual, "The Social Relationships Class", or another name reflecting the special purpose.

The class (5–7 students) has its own room, large enough to provide space between the children. The colors are calm, no distracting or moving objects. Cell phones, Game Boys and similar items are not allowed in class, or are kept in the teacher's drawer.

The classroom interior is always the same. Everything is positioned towards the teacher's seat. Everything has a specific place, and the quality of materials is so good that it is natural to take good care of them. Anything broken is immediately repaired or replaced. At least one teacher is with the children when they are on the playground.

There are not necessarily many teachers (one or two during the day), but the resources should suffice. There is a certain degree of isolation from the rest of the school/world, and any contact with the outside environment is planned. The class can be situated in a normal school, but should be regarded as an independent organization sharing facilities and certain events with the rest of the school.

The teachers report directly to the school principal or board of directors. The teachers should be motivated for a long-term work (3 years at least), and not be too young or inexperienced. The teachers accept their role as "successful parents" besides their usual teacher role. The teachers accept that the children are more or less emotionally handicapped and that they may never become "normal". The task is to help them live with their handicaps and learn as much as possible.

Anyone working with or affiliated with the team is willing to cooperate and spend time on team building. Usually, the time span for developing a stable organizational culture is 3–5 years, with many disappointments along the way.

In my experience as a supervisor, these are the realistic terms that must be met in order to keep an acceptable frustration level for those who engage in this difficult task.

Results

Even children with severe criminal records and emotional handicaps can function amazingly well after time spent in this kind of setting. This does not necessarily mean that they are maturing, but that you are providing exactly the setting needed for this specific problem. Don't let the progress in class create the illusion that the child is "healed" miraculously. You will often find that a lack of structure outside of class elicits immediate regression in behavior patterns.

Most important the setting provides a secure base, sufficient to use the child's cognitive resources for learning to read and write, rather than for defending itself in energy consuming ways.

End of Classroom Section.

CHAPTER 11

DAILY LIFE IN THE FAMILY, THE FOSTER FAMILY OR THE INSTITUTION

As the AD child grows up, the gap between the social performance of the child and normal developing children becomes evident. Normal children are able to cope with groups of adults and develop bonds between each other. The AD child is often alone. It may have many acquaintances but no long term friendships. Challenges for learning and socializing are avoided instead of approached, and often incomprehensible emotional expectations can make the child retreat to isolation or fight/flight behavior. The attitude of other children towards the AD child will often be admiration (on behalf of risk-taking and disobedient behavior from the AD child) and fear (caused by threatening, dominating or aggressive behavior and occasionally including sexual misconduct).

At home, the intimacy of family life can trigger the AD child's behavior problems which can cause burnouts and feelings of burnout in other members of the family. In fact, the very intimacy that causes us to create families can wake the "sleeping lion" in the child (early unconscious experiences of neglect and anger). Many families often try to "reach the child" by trying to create an even closer relationship which in turn provokes the early working models of the child even more.

Goals

Give the child a stable and structured environment. Minimize the frequency and severity of conflicts.

Adjust parental behavior to match the emotional and cognitive capacity of the child. Protect other children in the family. Monitor the social relationships of the family in order to avoid rejection of the AD child from the local community and extended family members.

Methods

The most common "Catch 22" in adoptive and foster families is that the parents make tremendous efforts to establish emotional interaction by increasing intimacy when problems arise. This is because "mutual intimacy" is the hallmark of successful parenting. The failure to achieve this must then mean "incompetent parenting". This idea is as common as it is wrong. The most important decision is to postpone the goal of intimacy in the beginning and realize that the child has an intimacy problem which will be amplified by direct assault on its protective defense mechanisms. If you ignore this problem and try to take shortcuts to love, the road will be longer. Splitting, projection and psychotic episodes are bound to follow.

You must postpone your own need for reconfirmation of your role as a parent or caretaker and start asking yourself what behavior is relevant and comprehensible to the child. The question is not, "How do I break through his/her armor?" The question is; "At what emotional distance does the child seem to be most comfortable and perform the best?"

First, divide the child's age by four. Then consider what meaningful parental behavior would be appropriate for a child this age. How many decisions would you leave to a child this age? Would you preach endlessly to a child that age when something went wrong? How long would you leave a child of that age alone and expect it to remember what you said? How long would you expect it to concentrate during a conversation or on homework? How well would you expect it to differentiate between truth and fantasy? Would you leave a child that age alone in a room where there are matches or lighters? Would you leave it with a younger sibling when jealousy was present?

A delay in emotional and social development means exactly this; you must change all your social behavior and communication style to attune with a much younger child.

Take away the burdens

Ask yourselves, when looking at the daily routine where and when is the child unable to understand our behavior, because we are parenting at a higher developmental level? Where does conflict repeat itself because we don't take control and do the obvious; make any sensible decision the child is unable to make? Where do we talk, discuss, argue, reprimand and persuade instead of following our own intuition and simply act in relevant ways without expecting agreement from the AD child? How often do we change the background (room, persons present, way of doing things, time schedules, bedside story, food, theme, groups)? How often do we challenge the child with two adults addressing it instead of one?

Take away the burdens from "the lost conqueror". The child may "win" single impulsive battles, you will always win in the long run. You are more patient, you are more insisting you are stronger and wiser. No matter what it says, the child can't live without your help.

Burden No. 1: having to decide, choose, argue, agree and feel motivated

Show (don't tell) the child that you are ready to make any decision that the child is unable to make. Tell the child what is going to happen now (dress, eat, brush teeth, go for a walk). See that it is done. Sit down and wait – and be ready to wait until the child comes to you on it's own. If, for example, the child won't eat, say how long the food will be on the table, stay seated, don't talk or encourage in any way. When time has run out: say in a calm way that you are taking away the food. Whatever the child says, accuses you of, appeals about, just state that you said the food was there for so long, and now that time is over. You serve many small meals during the day since children thrive better that way, but whenever you serve anything; sit down at the table and say how long the food will be there. Don't change the food choices if the child refuses to eat.

You can measure your own trustworthiness by a simple equation; are you running after the child, or is the child running after you? You should be the (immobile) center of the child's world.

Don't present choices to the child, present your own decisions. If the child challenges your decision, say; "You don't have to think it's a good idea, you don't have to want to do it. That's okay. I have decided that it is best"

Don't expect the child to agree, expect the child to disagree and know that you must do it anyway. Keep your doubts to yourself; doubts must be dealt with alone or with other leaders, such as your spouse. Children with AD do not give adequate responses, so all decisions are based on your own solitary judgment. The more you discuss, the less you can be trusted as a figure who is stronger than the child's anxiety.

If you are part of a group or family working with the AD child; never change, overrule or discuss any decision presented to the child by another adult in front of the child. No matter how wrong you find it, it can only be discussed later on the strategy meeting. During the day; let one person be the leader and decision maker in the eyes of the child.

Don't expect the child to feel motivated, pleased or happy about your plans. If the child didn't learn this as a baby, you should act using your own enthusiasm without expecting the same in return.

Burden No. 2: background changes

As described early, an immature constancy function means that any background change or unexpected change will make the child's focus – and gestalt of what is going on – collapse on the spot.

Make the whole day a series of short routine rituals. Do the same things at the same time in the same room and in the same tone of voice. Keep you creative, impulsive and spontaneous ideas to yourself. Perform the same activity schedule every week. If you bought a new hat and a new makeup, don't wear it when you meet the child.

Don't do anything new without preparing the child in advance. Don't get out of the car at the supermarket before you have told the child where we are going, what you will see, how to behave and to stay by your side all the time. Don't start going to bed without telling the child all that will happen before sleeping. Before sleep, talk to the child about what will happen the next day, and repeat this again in the morning during breakfast.

Your child is vulnerable to any change. Present what will happen, wait for the overload reaction and then repeat the plan again.

Tell guests how to behave in the same routine manner when visiting. Tell them that if the child asks them anything, they should say "Mom or Dad knows that/decides that/plans that. Ask them". Do not have friends and relatives visiting who are not able understand this. Give a short explanation about the child's problem to anyone you meet. Don't hesitate to do this, don't expect people to agree or understand. Explain your conditions for being together with friends and family.

If you must have a surprise party, make sure that the AD child is not in the house. Under no circumstances plan a surprise party for the child's birthday.

Whenever you are in new situations (entering a shop, meeting new people or children), let the child walk, sit next to you, and even hold your hand. Talk about what "we see from here", to help the child conceptualize and frame what is going on in this situation. Create a "parent/child circle" as a base of any excursions.

If a major change is about to happen (moving, another setting, starting school) do not introduce the change until shortly before the change is about to happen, perhaps only a few days prior. Any unknown future possibilities and speculations will consume all the energy of the child. Think about what happens in a company where "rumors of change from the top" are circulating. Even if you are in doubt about the consequences of a change, present the future as a number of facts.

Burden No. 3: complex social relationships and interactions

Socializing for the emotionally young does *not* mean socializing with other children. It means "Share simple and clear emotions, by touch and eye contact, inside the caretaker/child "magic circle', never disturbed by intruders".

When giving the child any direction, be sure to touch it (hold hands, a hand on the shoulder) and make it look at you. Don't tell it anything before you sense some attention to what you are going to say. Wait calmly until the child has surmounted its resistance towards contact. Follow up and help the child complete your direction.

Let the mother/child magic circle be there even if you are with other people. Don't allow the child to leave it unless you have agreed where it will go and when it will return to you. Whenever the child returns, give a small reward like, "That was good". If the child does not return, bring it back "Oh, I shouldn't have let you go, that cake looked so good and that was too difficult for you".

Make yourself the safe center for short explorations. Practice; "agreeing, leaving for a short while to explore something, come back and talk about it". Give the child a bracelet or a watch with a picture of you to talk to while it is "away". Or, give the child a cell-phone and be in constant communication while it is exploring or doing something in the kitchen while you sit on the porch, relaxed and interested.

Burden No. 4: being blamed or reprimanded when something goes wrong

Whatever goes wrong or the child does wrong, even if you know the child had intended to sabotaging your plan, just say you were not there to help it. The instruction you gave was too difficult for the child. You had not taken into account how angry he or she was. You exposed the child to too much change.

Anything that goes wrong is *your* responsibility (don't feel guilty about it; it just happens with the immature or young child). Gradually, you can direct the child's attention to another fact; "You know it's funny; things only go wrong when I'm not there, did you notice that?" You will become inevitable and indispensable in a few months.

When something goes right, give your kind appreciation; "You are learning now".

In this setting, it is not possible for the child to do anything wrong!

It takes time to develop yourself into a brand new, unaffected and kind person every morning. Find somewhere to recreate yourself, a therapist, your spouse (have container dumping meetings every evening), or friends. Realize that you are under siege, get fresh water from the outside.

Burden No. 5: parents or caretakers leaning on the accelerator

Slow down. If you read a bedtime story, try and read more slowly. Pause and focus on each new event: "Once upon a time there was a prince; *do you know what a prince looks like?* Well, this prince lived with his father because his mother had died, *oh, poor thing! No mother! What do you think it would be like living without a mother?* Well, anyway, he lived in castle, etc." Read the same story 20 nights in a row.

Slow down. Doing one thing with concentration is better than doing ten things without. Make a list of what you should do with and for the child today, eliminate eight out of ten and do the remaining two items as well as you can.

Postpone developmental challenges or institutional changes as long as possible. Stay in preschool for an extra year. Play with one other child at a time always with a parent present.

Accept that the delay in development becomes more noticeable as the child increases in age.

By remaining consistent without ever arguing, being the center for exploration and the container of all burdens, the child can feel safe. And this is the necessary premise for learning everything you should learn from age 5–11.

When you have created a safe haven for the child, with this approach, it is time to teach the child how to cope with everyday problems.

How to acquire new skills in six steps

A baby will learn by means of imitating parental behavior. Perhaps this is what annoys you with your child "No matter where we are she can anticipate the wishes of the other person and imitate his or her behavior, everybody finds her so charming" Well, this is perfectly natural infant behavior and a natural adult response to infant behavior patterns!

Far from being annoyed, you should realize that this behavior is the key to interaction and the gateway to mutual learning circles.

Any normal baby will imitate the behavior of its mother and have no idea why we do this or that. The reason for imitating anything is because mother does it. It is only much later that the baby will start grasping the meaning and the practical purpose of the behavior.

Therefore, when practicing any skill you should follow the sequences below. Don't continue to the next sequence before you are sure that the child has mastered previous one. Focus on one skill at a time.

The skill to be learned must be simple and short, such as, "drawing a person", "putting on a shirt", "washing your hands", "playing ball", or whatever skill you think may be useful in daily situations.

Start with a skill the child is already able to perform, just to make the new situation a comfortable and successful environment. Don't stop just because of a few mistakes in the beginning, it takes time to become competent with the learning sequence. You may start with playing imitation games and offer a small prize at the end of each game. Some examples are, imitations of facial expressions, waving your hand, etc. If eye contact is difficult for the child, look just above or below the face and encourage the child to look at what you are doing.

First sequence: mirroring your behavior here and now

1. Place yourself in front of the child at approximately the distance of an outstretched arm. You may vary the distance to find the optimum.
2. Tell the child what "we" are now going to do.
3. Tell the child to do what you do (at the same time).
4. Do what you want the child to do and help it imitate your movements.

Second sequence: your voice as the organizer of behavior

Gradually move less and less, and at the same time start "thinking aloud", telling the child what it is doing while it tries to do the movement. "Now I turn on the cold water, now I turn on the hot water, now is it too hot? I must turn up the hot water a little more, this feels good, now I reach for the soap, oops, it is slippery, I hold it with both hands now, etc."

Third sequence: the childs voice as the organizer

Encourage the child to gradually do the activity while you are still in front of it, but you gradually stop moving, remain visible and passively interested, and let the child instruct itself in the sequences of e.g. "washing hands" by talking out loud about what it is doing.

Fourth sequence: working in parallel positions

Do the activity while you are no longer in front of the child, but beside it. Still working in simultaneous movement, and gradually you are more and more passive, though still interested and paying attention.

Fifth sequence: being out of sight

Every time the child is performing the activity, you gradually move further away. Every time the child does not succeed you move closer again. If necessary, encourage the child with your voice.

Sixth sequence: I can do it on my own!

Start doing something else for short periods while the child is performing the activity. Encourage the child to whisper instead of talking out loud. Gradually encourage the child to not vocalize at all, but to "say it to yourself". You may whisper yourself while doing something. Start eliminating the detailed instructions and use the general instructions, like "Wash your hands now". Start leaving the room for short periods, you may have a picture of yourself hanging on the bathroom mirror to help the child maintain object permanence. Stand in the next room and talk to the child, "You can't see me now, can you? Can you still remember what I said?"

These six steps should be applied to the learning of all daily tasks. Once you and the child become familiar with the sequence, you will

I encourage the participants to openly reflect on the emotional states and motivations for the actions of themselves and those of important attachment figures in their life. This method is inspired by the "mentalizing" methods developed by Fonagy (Fonagy 1999) and others. The ability to reflect on motives and emotions is a quality in people who have a secure and autonomous attachment pattern, and is supposed to play an important role in the ability to control emotions. Children who have experienced early maltreatment or abuse do not develop this capacity very well and have a poor understanding of the motives and feelings of others.

In therapy, I often start with an "emotional mapping" process, asking both caretakers and youth to describe openly the present feelings of the AD youth towards his or her actual caretakers (instructing the caretakers not to comment, argue or discuss these feelings). Ambivalent and contradictory feelings are especially explored and identified (such as feeling dependence and hatred simultaneously). I ask the youth to describe these feelings to *me*, while the parents are listening, otherwise the process may end in conflict. Great care is taken to have all feelings described in detail, including the situations that trigger them the most. The descriptions will often revolve around basic social themes, such as feeling excluded from the family, being dominated by the caretakers, and not having emotional needs met.

The two mechanisms, regression and the projection, of early "working models" are then explained in detail with practical examples from what the youth has just said. He or she is "talking to the (biological) parents who once were not what they should be", and the consequent difficulties of seeing "Those who are present now". The (much despised) reactions of the present parents are described to the youth as essentially the same: the youth is back in the past, and this causes the parents to make regression to their own past (times when they as children were bullied, victimized or maltreated). The conclusion:

You talk to your "parents who once were", and your parents talk to their "parents who once were". The aim of these sessions is that you and your parents find out how to talk directly without interference from the "ghosts" of long past unfortunate parenting. You both have a right to be angry for what you did not receive, but this anger belongs to other times and parents and should not be allowed to interfere with your relationship. Until now, only three unhappy children are quarrelling.

I then ask the parents individually to describe how they were raised and what was lacking or destructive to their security or autonomy. I ask them to describe where they react towards the youth as their own parents did to them. Other important losses, such as not having a biological child of their own, are also explored, if these losses interfere with the relationship with the AD youth.

In the session, the participants can make a map by painting themselves and their actual parent/youth relationship in the middle. Above them the "once were" parents, dictating what should be said, done and felt in the actual relationship. I ask the participants to study how the patterns of the negative "once were" parenting is supported and continued in the actual dialogue between parents and youth. I give feedback whenever I hear a clear statement emerging from the present relationship and take a humorous attitude towards "old relationship" patterns. The aim is to make the parents and youth recognize how they maintain the "lonely child" dialogue and when they are able to act from a more mature position. All setbacks are defined as temporarily "needing the good old cradle again".

I ask the youth and parents to address the "once were parents" on the drawing and tell them what they did right and wrong, while expressing relevant feelings (anger, sadness, abandonment, longing).

I then describe the process of conception, being nurtured, raised and becoming independent as "painting a picture together", a contin-ued process of dialogue between parents and child, ending with the youth finishing the painting alone when entering adulthood. In the actual case (with a discontinued early childhood full of loss, lack of care and constantly changing "parents"), the work is much more difficult. Rather than painting, it is like trying to put together a puzzle of very different events and contributions to the life of the child. The pieces of the puzzle don't fit into each other immediately, they even come from different puzzles, and some are missing completely. This means that the child had to adjust itself to many different parental styles/languages/settings early in life, and some of the support neces-sary to mature was missing completely.

The aim of this dialogue is to create respect in the child and parents for the problems of creating a unified sense of identity, based on evidence. Some of the common scenarios:

– You were almost dying from lack of food and drink and you responded by finding smart ways to survive. When placed in the foster family, you were not allowed to use all your knowledge about survival (scream, lie, steal, bite, etc.).
– You had no love from anyone, and suddenly others were disap-pointed if you didn't love them immediately.

It is important to notice that the AD child is almost a possible abuser from an early age by lacking sensitivity to the needs and boundaries of other people, a tendency towards indiscriminate imitation of any behavior and impulsive and uninhibited behavior. Many AD children have experienced early abuse prior to treatment or placement and have not developed normal limits to sexual behavior.

The purpose of treatment will therefore also be to protect children and others in their environment against trauma and abuse caused by the child/juvenile. As an example, as a supervisor in an institution I have experienced, that it was very difficult for staff in to keep a group of 7–9 year old AD children from trying to have rather radical "sex" with each other, regardless of gender. Another example: an 11 year old AD girl is approached by a boy from the community. He asks in a timid way if she wants to date him. And she replies: "Oh sure, let's go over in the barn and fuck". His parents were not pleased.

As the topic of AD and sexual abuse has not been described in literature, the following relies on my limited professional experience regarding possible treatment. The serious problem is that the professional or parent often meets the child long after the abuse was initiated and became part of the child's lifestyle.

The AD child also has the double role of being a potential abuser (towards other children) and a victim of abuse (from an adult), the dual roles being rooted in the same quality, a lack of critical sense and boundaries towards others. For this reason, being both abused and exerting abuse towards others is discussed in this section. The difference is a question of age, as abused AD children often develop into abusers later in life.

What are the important goals when working with abused AD children?

Preventing possibilities for abuse

One apparently obvious measure is to stop the continued abuse. This is not as simple as it seems.

The AD child or youth may actively try to seek contact with the abuser who may offer money or other rewards The child may abuse other children whenever there is any opportunity, in short it takes a lot of manpower to avoid situations where abuse is possible. The abuser may be a parent where it can be a legal problem to deny any contact that is not supervised by a social worker or therapist. This is often the case since abuse is often suspected, but can't be proved legally.

When caring for the abused AD child it is important to be present whenever the child is with other children, especially younger or weaker children. It is also necessary to inform other caretakers in an honest and matter-of-fact way that the child can be abusive and supervision must be present at all times. Ultimately, incarceration can be the only means of protecting others, particularly when the abusing child reaches puberty.

Helping staff cope with abuse problems

It can be very frustrating for staff members to be sexually intimidated by children or youth, or accused of sexual abuse and having to return children to their parents when abuse is suspected. This may cause an air of paranoia in the staff and a tendency towards an excessive "safeguarding distance", harming the relationship with the child. Regular external supervision is therefore imperative, and at least two staff members should be working together with the child documenting any events in writing.

The attachment element; be stronger than the abuser in the eyes of the child

Negative bonding (where the child is afraid of the attachment person) is unfortunately just as effective as positive bonding, an overlooked fact in attachment studies. In my experience the only effective treatment of a child bonding with an abuser is to offer an even stronger bond to a professional. This can be an emotional bond, but with severe AD and a reduced capacity for bonding the child should experience the professional social worker as being stronger, and consistently more in control than the abuser, thus offering a safer haven. This also requires close professional supervision with the case manager.

Setting behavior limits: what can you do where?

With the abusive AD child, explanations and arguments are of little value. Setting clear standards for what to do and what is not allowed, is necessary. In the abovementioned example from an institution, the only effective intervention was to explain in detail to the children what was permitted and what was not, and then be present to help them behave normally. This may seem overly controlling, but the normal behavior helped the children to be accepted in other settings.

CHAPTER 14

THE PERSONAL DEVELOPMENT
OF THE AD CARETAKER

Introduction

The success of your efforts with the AD child or juvenile rests on your ability to withstand the impact of the early emotional "working model of a parent" in the child. In other words, the client has little idea of who he or she is, contains a lot of hostile concepts and has only a vague sense of personal borders and identity. So, you must know or rather feel exactly who you are, what you want, where your own borders are, what your purposes and goals are, and be able to practice them unaffected by "ups" or "downs" or "good days" and "bad days".

Feel like an angel, but act like a freight train.

This goes for the individual, the group and the organization. I have already said a lot about how to organize daily settings – in the classroom, at home, etc. Here, I shall turn to the problem of internal organization in the individual therapist and the staff.

Developmental phases of the individual AD worker and objectives for the supervision process

Based on my experiences in supervising people of various professions and family members, there seems to be some common traits in the personal development of those who stay with the job long enough to become experienced professionals. Usually the personal development process will take 2–5 years. Some characteristics of the personal maturation process are described below.

State of the magic wand

The supervisee meets the child without having previous experience of AD. The reactions to the child's problems are: to reinforce the person's normal social contact strategies behavior and knowledge about normal personality and attachment development. The person does the natural thing: tries to make a deeper connection.

This very natural impulse challenges the low emotional capacities of the AD child, eliciting fight/flight or manipulation or withdrawal from the child. In this phase denial of the child's problem, finding excuses in other circumstances (his parents are SO bad!). Fantasies of personal therapeutic omnipotence are common. For example, "I'm the only one who understands him, nobody else does! I'll get behind his shell to his heart with *my* method", etc.

The supervisee's general working model of others is shaken, and his or her self-concept is threatened, resulting in a reinforcement of the person's usual coping strategy, and not a change of strategy. In normal social relationships, we maintain our self and identity assisted by normal feedback from others. When we receive confusing and inconsistent feedback from a person, our sense of self is disturbed.

This state can last for years if the capacity for emotional involvement or professional orientation is a strong part of the supervisee's identity.

Early personal attachment trauma may be the drive of the professional's efforts, and consequently the healing of the child becomes a "life or death" project since it is really an effort to also heal the person's own early experiences. The supervisee partly sees herself in the child, and not the child as it is. The child quickly realizes that it can control you by responding to, or denying response to, your narcissistic need for external reconfirmation and success.

Objectives for the supervisor

If you are a supervisor for a primary case manager in this state it is necessary to show full acceptance of the "working model" of that person and pay respect to a life strategy which has worked out so far. You may enter a mapping process of early experiences and how the persons own working model was created. The supervisee can write a diary concerning the outcome of various contacts with the child during the day.

The supervisee will often be very projective, i.e. almost obsessed with what the child is doing, thinking and feeling – and not very aware what he or she is doing, feeling or thinking as a professional. You may gently turn that persons attention to a regular observe their own reactions, and try to stretch the persons time perspective by pointing out patterns in the child's and the supervisees interactions.

You may point out that it is natural to experience anxiety when your basic notions are at stake. As a defense mechanism, the supervisee will often feel that "You don't understand this child/don't see his capacities", which means "I'm afraid that you don't understand me". The supervisee can alternate between helplessness "Tell me what to do, you're the expert" and rejection of the supervisor "You told me to do this or that, and it doesn't work at all – you're the one who is incompetent!".

At this time, you should provide a secure and accepting environment for the supervisee who will be very vulnerable in the transformation process of revising basic notions and self-concepts.

State of reality depression

The supervisee begins to think that all efforts are in vain. In fact, whatever the person tries only seems to make things worse. The person is unconsciously taking over the defense mechanisms of the child (denial, rejection, splitting, projective identification, low self-esteem, incompetence, abandonment, etc.). This may be detrimental to social relationships (colleagues, family, others in care of the child, spouse, etc.), and the person may become over-responsible, suspicious, reject external support and care, have numerous conflicts because he or she feels let down and misunderstood by others. Negative feeling towards the child may be projected towards others in order to maintain the relationship to the child. Various camouflages are used to avoid the basic feeling of self-pity and abandonment.

This is a point where some give up in order not to fall apart. That's okay. The child will not profit from seeing a caretaker give up. Just remember to tell the child that "I am not strong enough to be your parent/therapist, and I will find someone who is". Don't use the child's behavior in that explanation.

One variant of feeling incompetent is the fantasy "There must be some therapeutic God out there who can heal him when I fail", and a quest for the miracle starts. In this phase the supervisee is an easy victim for illusionists who are after money or admiration and dependency – or both. And of course, there are some who just want to offer their professional help.

Those able to endure this frustrating period have begun realizing the true capacities of the child and succeed in separating their own emotional needs from those of the child. The supervisee starts foreseeing the child's pattern during interactions rather than feeling 3 steps behind. The person may live through the grief of realizing the child's handicaps in a process of active resignation. This means that the real capacities and useful working points will stand out clearly – how the person can help the child develop on its own terms in some areas.

Objectives for the supervisor

Here you must help the person make a realistic evaluation of whether he or she is able to work with AD children, and possibly explore how the person can use their skills elsewhere. People with fine emotional and social skills who are sensitive can be of more value to normal children. You should plan a thorough evaluation process in order to avoid a sudden desperate decision followed by guilt and inferiority feelings. If the person is an adoptive parent or foster family member, the issue may be the child's placement in an institution in order to save the family, or marital conflict issues triggered by the behavior of the AD child.

In the resignation process of the supervisee, your authority will often be challenged, and the person may look for other authorities presenting more optimistic prospects. At the same time, the supervisee should be made aware that he or she is beginning to develop professional views and the ability to master many situations with the child. You should guide the person into summarizing where basic notions of personality have changed, how the person has become able to foresee the outcome of different interactions with the child (what works and what doesn't), and how the separation process ("The child and I are two separate people") causes both relief and sadness.

Gaining authority and internal reorganization

The supervisee starts understanding the child and is able to be with it without identifying emotionally with it. The person is able to tolerate the slow development of the child and respect it. Consequently the person is of value, becoming a stabilizing factor. The

Another issue to be resolved is the "background problem"; we are all members in other groups also, and we may feel more obliged to them than to this emerging group. The question of different professional backgrounds will surface; if the group consists of teachers, doctors, students, members from religious organizations, etc.; members may fear that one profession or value might set the basic agenda for the group as a whole and that the group is exposed to "hostile takeover" from one of the member's professional group. In the foster family the problem may be whether the AD child is the most important priority in the family, or whether male or female norms of upbringing should rule. Are we a normal family or a family with a child that is quite different from us? For example, adoptive families often try to maintain that the adopted child is "just another family member who should live by the same set of rules and norms" in order to achieve a high degree of inclusion. This may be detrimental to both the family as well as the AD child who has quite different backgrounds and competences.

If the group succeeds in creating commitment, a sense of basic mutual trust will establish, and an air of "we're just so good and so much better than other groups" will be present for a period of time. A set of more or less unspoken rules of conduct will appear and the members will refer to the group as "we". Everyone in the group will feel equal and responsible and the experienced need for leadership will be minimal.

Leadership in this phase will be the role of "the good host/hostess"; to invite relevant (and only the relevant) professionals to participate in the group, to make each member feel respected and included into the group, to speak openly about the problems of being a member of other groups as well, and discuss how the individual members can cope with that problem. To validate that there may be differences in degree of commitment, to define the bottom line for necessary engagement/obedience to group norms and to define what is relevant and what is not.

If the emotional pressure from the child's/children's AD problems is too intense, the group might continue without a common ground and basic trust, or simply dissolve. It might also retreat to a defensive position by taking the "we" too far (rigid norms), reconfirming how "fantastic we are", or discussing new projects without any signs of practical work and openness towards the environment. The group may form dependency towards the leader and try to avoid personal responsibility by relying on a "supernaturally strong person".

Control: realizing that we are different from each other

Having formed a base, the group will work on the problems of control; influence, power, decision making, authority, competences and working roles. The group is working to find an appropriate way of establishing a vertical structure, some gain more influence than others, some are active and some are passive, some talk and some communicate with silence.

Differences between members become increasingly obvious and start consuming their thoughts. We don't have the same values/age/experience/gender/methods/attitudes towards work/need for power, etc. The problem is whether we can talk about it openly? The group will have fantasies about basic trust disappearing if differences and conflicts are brought up. There will be a lot of discussion about borders; who should do what, who can decide what, how we make decisions at all, if this is this your job or mine, etc. Former unconscious experiences of abuse of power, or inability to influence others may present themselves.

Subgroups may form and make alliances to gain influence or exclude others.

If the group manages to discuss differences in the open, a number of confrontations will take place, and members will occupy different positions and roles.

Members will gradually find their preferred role and spend a lot of energy on protecting it and gaining acceptance from the group. Basic roles are:

The structure leader ("Let's get things done"). The person in this position will be aware of how and when things should be done, create plans and time schedules and request the establishment of working routines. The usual fear in this person will be that others might reject him or her because of emotional incompetence.

The emotional leader ("How do you feel about that?") This person will be concerned with emotional issues and openness and be sensitive to conflict and power play in the group. This person may fear rejection for being too absorbed, and losing the ability to oversee and plan, and may fear being "too much" in the eyes of others.

The opposition leader ("On the contrary, I think ...") This person will doubt decisions and suggest alternatives, or try to import the methods and attitudes of external groups. This person may fear being rejected from the group as being stubborn, or too sensitive.

The stability leader ("Oh, well"). This person is generally unwilling to change, referring to past experience as an argument. The person will question the value of anything new or view it as another variation of the known. This person will fear becoming too included in the group, losing personal independence.

The guardian leader ("I told you this would go wrong"). This person will try to protect the group by anticipating any dangers or loss of control, and constantly worry about consequences. This person will fear rejection from his or her inability to relax and being seen as too critical towards other members.

These roles are, at the same time, a strength and menace to the group, until it figures out how to handle them. They hold the promise of group versatility in resolutions and interactions with clients.

Leadership in this phase will be twofold: to contain the negative emotions and anxieties, and to "stay on the horse" since the group will project internal conflicts as a team/leader conflict. All leader decisions will be questioned, ignored and doubted. The leader will be seen as "too soft/too tough and insensitive". The task is to find ways of, talking matter-of-fact, about differences and how to cope with them, being open about conflicts in the group and staying with decisions already made. If the leader gives in, takes criticism too personal, or becomes a "negotiator", the group will lose confidence and be unable to control internal anxiety.

The prevailing defense mechanism in this phase will be splitting, and the group may reduce itself to a fight/flight group. Needless to say, the AD child will be able to create a lot of disruption in the group process at this phase, since it has the same defense mechanism. Therefore, the leader must also help the group form a mutual and effective communication system ("what did the child say to whom?"). Some AD children are master group consultants, albeit in a negative way.

The group may also avoid processing differences and develop into an "It's so nice to be together" group, high on inclusion and intimacy and low on decision making, time schedules and direction. If so, the leader should not accept that he or she is the only one responsible for the structure.

In this phase the group will be very productive, but members will have a tendency to work in different directions at the same time (egocentric role administration).

Openness/affection – mutual exchange

Due to the previous work of conflict and confrontation, the group member now has an internal map of organization; each member knows how the others will react emotionally and practically towards any new task, and the individuals know the limits of their own competences and tasks.

The group is now ready to find out how open they should be and how much is relevant to share with each other. They need to find an appropriate degree of formal, personal or intimate exchange. The issue is closeness and distance.

Conflicts will revolve around this theme, some may think that others are too secluded and do not share enough with the group, others may feel uncomfortable if challenged to be more open than they like to be. Vulnerability will be the issue.

Working with AD children is often a very personal endeavor and this may increase sensitivity to criticism (is this personal or professional?) and activate basic patterns of attachment.

As pointed out by adult attachment studies started by Hazan and Shaver (1987), our basic attachment style seems to be relatively stable and considerably influences our adult way of socializing. What will emerge in this phase are the basic styles and emotions in each member. Mixtures of dependence and avoidance emerge; some members are preoccupied with relationships, some are secure, some are dismissing, some are fearful.

The group searches for a way to recognize and accept these differences in attachment style. If the group succeeds, personal relationships and subgroups will form, but this time they will not be negative alliances, but rather appropriate "common interest" groups. Members can have a humorous and forgiving attitude towards their own limitations and characteristics; the tone is not sarcastic, but warm and accepting.

Leadership: Help members accept different needs for intimacy. Recognize different attachment styles and attachment problems in the group and define them as resources and valuable professional knowledge for understanding the AD clients. Prevent relationships exceeding the appropriate degree of intimacy in the working group. Keep the professional aspect of the work in the forefront. Help members prevent getting so emotionally involved in the work or colleagues that they ignore their private life.

If distance is the problem, the leader can take up problems of openness, personal problems and intimacy.

Help the group develop feedback systems where the line between personal feedback and professional feedback is clear to all participants.

CHAPTER 16

METHODS FOR THE AD TEAMWORK

Some tools for team development

Daily life must be designed in a way that gives staff members space and time to talk about and share their reactions to the AD children's behavior. This can be done through professional supervision from an outside psychologist, but it basically relies on the group's own initiative to create a positive working climate. For your inspiration, here are some exercises you can use to enhance openness in the group. Use the ones that seem to respond to your actual needs:

Mapping "attachment knowledge" in the team

A good way for team members to get acquainted is by creating a resource map through the following interview. You can start in pairs and then share by table if the group is large. It is worth the while to spend a whole day on this activity. In smaller groups, six or less, everyone can share.

The purpose of the interview is to give each member the opportunity to express and discover what his or her basic assumptions are for understanding AD children. This can only be done by looking at your own "early working models", your early experiences. Eventual traumatic experiences are a resource because they are a key to empathy with the AD child, and a key to understanding your own emotional motivation for entering this kind of work. The more aware you become of how your early experiences and reactions formed your personality, the more valuable they will be in your work.

You may not know the answer to all the questions. If not, answer based on your intuition.

1. *What were the general circumstances of your parents during the time when your mother was pregnant with you? Do you know the attitudes of your parents towards having a child? How old were your parents then? What were their resources?*
2. *What was your birth weight and how did the labor proceed? Was it a difficult birth?*
3. *What was your general reaction pattern after birth – your temperament – how did you thrive? What stories have you heard about what you were like?*
4. *Do you know if you experienced any physical separation periods from your mother before age three?* (confined to an incubator, mother's illness or absence, being hospitalized, etc.)? If so, do you know how you reacted to this experience?
5. *What is your first memory of separation/loss from parents or loved ones?* How did this experience influence basic feelings such as trust, anger, grief, independence?
6. *What is your first memory of feeling close, loved, accepted, attached?* How did this experience influence basic items such as self-reliance, belief, hope, trust, frustration tolerance?
7. *When you are in emotional or stressful situations today, how do you react?* Anger, withdrawal, insecurity, detached from your feelings, self-blame and shame. What is your coping pattern?
8. *Where did these early experiences make you stronger and resilient, where did they make you vulnerable?*
9. *Please sum up what you think are the resources (from coping with separation in your own early childhood) that enable you to understand the AD child.*
10. *How can you use your early experiences in your professional work without imposing your own life and resolutions on the AD child?*

After the small group interview session, the participants can sum up their experiences and reaction patterns on a whiteboard to illustrate the "personal knowledge pool" in the group: this is what we have learned about loss and separation in our lives. Discussions can take place around subjects such as:

– How can we make this knowledge pool useful in our daily work with AD children?
– Where do we recognize our own reaction patterns in those of the clients?
– How did these experiences cause learning problems and social problems, and how did they make us develop new faculties/strengths? How can we transfer this knowledge to our work?

The big ear

Once or twice a week the group practices The Big Ear. One person monitors the time. Each participant has exactly 5 minutes to talk about whatever emotions, reactions or thoughts have surfaced while working with the child. The remaining participants are not allowed to say anything or utter sounds of agreement/disagreement; they should try to listen with attention and care. If the person is silent after two minutes, they still have 3 minutes left to see if anything else emerges. The next person has 5 minutes, and so on. After the listening session, a free group discussion with 5 minutes for each of the following items is facilitated by the time-taker:

1. *If we look at what was said during the group sharing, what is the state of the group in general?*
   It is important that any personal statement is understood as an expression of something that is going on *in the group*. If one has expressed anger, there is anger in the group. The participants must learn to take responsibility for all feelings expressed in the group. It is of minor importance who expressed them.
2. *What happened between us and the child/children that brought up these emotions/thoughts? What experiences and reactions from our own childhood were activated?*
   Only the individual participant can do this interpretation. Participants should never interpret each other.
3. *How can we describe what is now happening in the group?*
   Do not try to come up with "solutions", rather take an interest in describing what is actually happening in the group, even if it seems negative at first glance.

If the time-taker experiences disrespect when announcing of time limits, they should express this immediately. The time limit structure reduces anxiety, so participants should support each other in respecting it.

The "mutual supervision" interview

If a child's behavior stirs up many emotional problems in caretakers, the following interview can be used in small groups (2 or 3 participants). The interviewer merely asks the questions and listens without commenting on the answers. Give enough time to answer after each question, takes notes and give the notes to the interviewed person afterwards. After the end of an interview (app. 45 minutes) roles are exchanged and a new interview is started.

1. What child/incident with a child do you want to talk about?
2. What feelings surface when you talk about it , describe them one by one, they can be conflicting feelings, pity, anger, resentment, irritation, whatever. Don't avoid negative feelings.
3. Where can you identify with the child? Is it based on your own childhood experiences?
4. When you are with the child, how do you repeat behavior patterns and reactions from your own childhood? Are they based on what you once did or felt or what your parents/adults did or felt?
5. How does your behavior determine the behavior of the child?
6. How can you change your own behavior in order to break the reaction pattern between you and the child?
7. If you try to see the child from "within", how would you describe the adults around you – try to use the words and tone of voice the child would use.
8. If you look at the child from a distant un-emotional position, how would you describe it?
9. Where is it difficult for you to be both detached and empathic towards the child?
10. What does the child do to make you respond in negative ways?
11. Where do you falter (lose your own intention/emotional state)?
12. How does that make you feel?
13. How are these feelings similar to those of the child?
14. Who do you allow to help you when work is difficult?
15. What thoughts/associations have surfaced during this interview?

If used regularly in difficult situations, this interview will gradually help the participants separate emotionally from the child, giving themselves freedom to choose even more professional attitudes and reactions instead of unconsciously being drawn into the child's conditions for contact.

Action learning – a tool for analysis and alternative solutions

This method is designed for the resolution of unresolved and Catch 22 situations. A problem owner and a time-taker are chosen. The person presenting a problem sits in front of a panel (4–6 persons) of participants without a table between them. A time monitor is chosen.

1. The person has 5 minutes to describe a problem with the child. The others listen, and take notes.
2. The panel members each have 5 minutes to write down what they think the problem is from their personal perspective (they should not accept the person's idea about what the problem is).
3. Each panel member has two minutes to describe to the group what they think is the major problem, 4–6 different definitions presented. At this time it is not permitted to suggest or hint at any proposals for solution. This is pure analysis of a problem. The person is silent and listens during the presentations.
4. Each member now has 5 minutes to write a suggestion for what the person can do to resolve the problem.
5. Each member has two minutes to present their suggestion to solve the problem. The person takes notes and listens.
6. The person tells the group what they heard and how this may have changed their idea about the problem or idea about what can be done.
7. Free discussion for 5 minutes.

There are two conditions that must be met if this exercise will present new ideas and actions; the participants must "dare to be different" in their analysis of what they see as being the problem and not become absorbed in the persons version. In steps 1–3 there must not be any suggestions for what to do, these steps are solely for analysis. When these terms are met, the exercise will often produce a host of new perspectives and good solutions.

Conclusion to organization of the therapeutic milieu

In a healthy organization for AD clients, focus will be on the creation of healthy individual and staff climate as well as on the clients. Milieu therapy is concerned with maintaining an environment that is able to provide mature and flexible psychological functions, enabling the AD child to perform and develop in everyday life. In order to achieve this goal, the organization must strive towards a high degree of emotional and organizational self-awareness.